EXODUS

UNDERSTANDING
THE
BASIC THEMES
OF
EXODUS

JOHN I DURHAM

WORD PUBLISHING
Dallas·London·Vancouver·Melbourne

EXODUS

Quick-Reference Bible Topics

Copyright © 1990 by Word, Incorporated. All rights reserved. No portion of this book may be reproduced in any form, except for brief quotations in reviews, without written permission from the publisher.

Unless indicated otherwise, quotations from the Bible in this volume are the author's own translation. Those from the book of Exodus are from the author's volume, Word Biblical Commentary/*Exodus*, vol. 3.

Library of Congress Cataloging-in-Publication Data

Durham, John I., 1933–
    Exodus / John I. Durham.
        p.   cm. — (Quick-reference Bible topics)
    Includes bibliographical references and index.
    ISBN 0-8499-3244-0
    1. Bible. O.T. Exodus—Criticism, interpretation, etc.
I. Title. II. Series.
BS1245.2.D87 1990
222'.1206—dc20   90-37368
                                          CIP

Printed in the United States of America
1 2 3 9 RRD 9 8 7 6 5 4 3 2 1

In grateful memory of
John Isaac and Lula Frances Durham
and
in glad appreciation of
Doc and DeDa Bailey,

Parentes Omnes

CONTENTS

FOREWORD

Finding the great themes of the books of the Bible is essential to the study of God's Word and to the preaching and teaching of its truths. These themes and ideas are often like precious gems: they lie beneath the surface and can only be discovered with some difficulty. Commentaries are most useful to this discovery process, but they are not usually designed to help the reader to trace important subjects systematically within a given book of Scripture.

This series, Quick-Reference Bible Topics, addresses this need by bringing together, within a few pages, all of what is contained in a biblical book on the subjects that are thought to be most significant to that book. A companion series to the Word Biblical Commentary, this series distills the theological essence of a book of Scripture as interpreted in the more technical series and serves it up in ways that will enrich the preaching, teaching, worship, and discipleship of God's people.

Exodus is an exciting, eventful book. John Durham's commentary on *Exodus* in the Word Biblical Commentary series (vol. 3) showed how the presence of God with his people is a major concern of the book of Exodus. Now he has moved beyond that to write about this and other features that make Exodus the important book that it is.

The preacher and the teacher, as well as earnest Bible students, will find insights here that will make reading, teaching, and preaching texts from Exodus easier and more meaningful. This can help make the Word of God "come alive."

Southern Baptist
   Theological Seminary
Louisville, Kentucky

John D.W. Watts
Old Testament Editor
Word Biblical Commentary
Quick-Reference Bible Topics

PREFACE

The completion in 1984 of my Word Biblical Commentary on *Exodus*, despite its bulk, left me still with things I wanted to say about this soaring second book in the Bible that is in thematic terms so fully the first book *of* the Bible. I felt myself wanting to provide, in a more compact form, a survey of the varied expressions of the central theological theme of the book of Exodus, the Presence of God in the life of his own people. I was also eager to share, in a brief and nontechnical presentation, a summary of the seven years of work presented in the translation, supporting notes, and commentary of that WBC *Exodus*. John Watts's invitation in May of 1988 to prepare this volume gave me the opportunity to do precisely that. (In these pages, when the Word Biblical Commentary volume is referred to, it will be identified as WBC 3—Word Biblical Commentary, Volume 3.)

As always, there are many to whom a debt of gratitude, far surpassing courtesy, must be extended. First and foremost, I must express my appreciation to, as well as for, my wife Betty, who was a partner in this writing as she is in every dimension of my life. Hers is a lovely companionship of nurture that engages every day of life as a gift that is brand-new.

To my caring congregation, the Greenwich Baptist Church, I am grateful for a measure of affirmation and trust that keeps me wanting to say and teach more this week than last week. And to my secretary Mrs. Marian Lein who typed all this from my penciled scribble while fulfilling a wide range of additional duties, I here record my thanks.

I have sought to provide, in the pages that follow, enough references to the text of Exodus to enable the reader to "keep the place"—my suggestion is that the biblical text be kept in one hand as this volume is read in the other hand. I have written in the hope that the reader might be guided in reading with understanding the text of Exodus, for which neither this book nor any other can ever be any substitute.

When Moses protested to Yahweh his limitations of articularity in the face of what he was expected to do in Egypt, Yahweh reminded him,

> "Who put a mouth on a man?
> Who makes him mute or deaf
>   or able to see or blind?
> Is it not I, Yahweh?
> Now get going. . . ."
>   (Exod 4:11, 12a)

I believe I know how Moses felt before this reminder. I know how he felt after it.

John I Durham
June 1989
Greenwich, Connecticut

1

THE THEME OF EXODUS:
GOD IS, HERE

The book of Exodus begins in the book of Genesis. There it is that Israel and his sons, faced with famine, travel down from Canaanland to the Delta of Egypt, where the good management of one of their own has created a surplus food bank. They journey without knowing that it is Joseph who will be their benefactor, without awareness that God has gone to Egypt before them all.

Joseph knows, and in due course he says to his brothers, "*You* did not send me here, it was God" (Gen 45:8), and "*you* had in mind harming me—God had in mind something good" (Gen 50:20). To Joseph, the dreamer, the incredible history of his life in Egypt amounted to more than fortunate coincidence. God had sent him ahead of the brothers as a means of snatching life from death (Gen 45:5), to preserve his people of purpose (Gen 45:7) for an undertaking of a proportion too vast for even Joseph to have dreamt. The scope of that undertaking is suggested in the call of Abraham (Gen 12:1-3). Its need is dramatized in the primeval history of Genesis 1–11 and powerfully presented by the open ending of the Babel story that concludes it (Gen 11:1–9). Its reason lies in God's patient passion for the human family he has made. Its end lies beyond anything Joseph, or even we ourselves, can have thought, and it will be in process as long as the human family continues its exciting and creative existence.

So it is that the book of Exodus continues the narrative of the book of Genesis by telling us what has occurred since Joseph expressed the wish, on his deathbed, that he be included in the trip back from Egypt to the land promised to his fathers, Abraham, Isaac, and Jacob. This return trip is simply assumed by Joseph as inevitable (Gen 50:22–26). The opening lines of the book of Exodus remind us, by repeating in summary form the genealogy of Genesis 46:8–27, that the story is now being continued. They refer also to the transition made inevitable by mortality, and report the fulfillment of God's promise of progeny making equally needful his parallel promise of land.

Such a continuation is remarkable enough as the story of a particular people, which it clearly is. Yet it is even more remarkable as a story of every people who suffer oppression and pain and the need of rescue. They are Israel, and so our ancestors in faith, these sons so carefully named. Their survival is at stake, we are soon to learn, in the narrative of the Pharaoh's attempt to manage them. But if we recall the universal beginning to the story so obviously being continued here, we have to recognize that these "seventy souls" are also us. As the poet of Deuteronomy 32:8 sings it,

"In the Supreme God's legacy to the nations,
    in His division of the sons of humankind,
He established the limits of the peoples
    correspondent to the counting of the Sons of Israel."

2   *EXODUS*

This remarkable statement, too often and incorrectly emended by translators and commentators at least from the time of the Septuagint, is entirely consonant with the ancient gazetteer of Genesis 10, which lists seventy nations as descendent from Shem, Ham, and Japheth, the three sons of Noah. The nations *before* Israel are counted as seventy, and here in Exodus, the book of Israel's birth, the nation *of* Israel is also counted, at its very foundation, as seventy.[1]

Thus the book of Exodus may be seen as a beginning begun already in the Book of Beginning, Genesis, and at the same time itself the beginning of a story that is even yet a long way from its end. For the book of Exodus is the beginning of the Old Testament, and therefore of the Bible; it is the account of the beginning of the nation of Israel, and therefore the account of the beginning of the kingdom of God—and the first confession of a coming of God that we Christians have come to call Incarnation.

There is an extensive range of literary form in the book of Exodus, from prose to poetry, from story to specification, from prayer to proclamation, from commandment to covenant formulary, from building plans to protocols of social behavior, from miracle-narratives to revelations of mystery, from etiology to ritual, from the characterization of humans to the description of the Divine. However, every sentence of it, even every syllable of it, has an incredibly unified theological purpose, a purpose that melds the most disparate components imaginable into a single, glorious whole, pulsating with a single confession.

This confession is made in every way imaginable: stated, then restated, declared, described, illustrated, symbolized, set forth in metaphor, in ritual, in story, in requirement, in architecture, in dialogue, in geographic terms, in promises, in disobedience and its consequences, in appearances and disappearances, in epiphany so awe-filling as to inspire flight and yet cause frozen immobility. Forty chapters of an almost infinite variety, the book of Exodus still has but a single end, and is just a series of variations on a single, simple theme. Every word of the forty chapters in some way serves that single, simple theme. All that is superfluous of it, or ancillary to it, has long since been worn away.

The book of Exodus is the farthest thing from a literary unity, a fact which every honest reader of its text has noticed since early in the Christian era, at least. One of the most fascinating aspects of the book is the way it tumbles over itself in its rush to declare its incredible good news, the manner in which it has been stretched apart here and there to make way for yet other sequences setting forth its point.

This literary diversity, indeed, has presented such a mare's nest to the source-form-tradition-redaction-canon critics that no two of them have proposed the same apportionment, or a common pedigree, for the theoretical pericopae of the book of Exodus.

Yet this complex collection of different-shaped and different-sounding literary pieces has been woven into one unvaried theological assertion, and the exposition of that assertion forms the insistent purpose of the book. That assertion, summed up in its simplest statement in the special covenant name of God, Yahweh (a name defined in the Old Testament only in this book) may be stated succinctly: God is here, or better still, God *is*, here.

The story of the book of Exodus is a story of God's Presence. Every turn of its ongoing narrative is a part of a cumulative confession of the palpable reality of His Nearness. The covenantal formulary of the book of Exodus is a response to God's Presence. Every general and particular requirement of its life-shaping obligation is a part of a studied response to the astonishing revelation that he has come to be with his people. The liturgical expectation of the book of Exodus is a reminder of God's Presence. Every word and every action of its ritual ceremony is a protocol of memory designed to keep Israel aware that he is always and immediately at hand. The architectural-implemental symbolism of the book of Exodus is a pictographic representation of God's Presence. Every material and each dimension of the Tabernacle, the furnishings within it and the space and the altar before it, are a prompting of sensory perception to the continuing signal, "He is here. He *is*, here."

Thus the book of Exodus is, in a remarkably singular way, a one-theme book of the Bible, a book that focuses a spectrum of theological confession, implication, and symbolism in the presentation of a single assertion of faith. Given the book's composite nature in literary source and form alone—not to mention its diverse liturgical, legal, and political interests—this uniformity of theological emphasis is almost incredible. Almost incredible, however, only until one remembers what the theological emphasis is. For the confession that God has come, and is here, is nothing less than the subject of the Bible, both Old Testament and New Testament alike. In a way, the book of Exodus anticipates all the rest of the Bible. And in a way, the book of Exodus may be taken as a symbol, perhaps even an anticipatory summary, of the major emphasis of the entire Bible.

I have sought elsewhere, in the Word Biblical Commentary *Exodus*, 1987, (henceforth called WBC 3) to demonstrate in detail how this is true. There,[2] I have suggested that the whole of the book of Exodus can be seen as an expression of "the theology of Yahweh present with and in the midst of his people Israel," a theme attested to by the narratives of Israel's rescue and by the provisions for Israel's response.

None of this is to suggest that the book of Exodus is not a complex tangle of traditions derived from the theological-literary legacy of many years and many contexts of need in many places. A cursory reading of the text of Exodus, even in English translation, is sufficient to establish that much, and the history of the literary-critical analysis of Exodus from the last quarter of the nineteenth century forward is a cumulative presentation of ever-smaller and more diverse pieces.

And yet we have the book in forty chapters that fairly cry out to be considered as a whole. Whatever we may notice in the way of repetition or inconsistency in these chapters, and however obvious may be the seams stitching the chapters together, the book of Exodus has a canonical form, a form in which it has been transmitted through the centuries, a form given it by theological *literati* whose interest was the confession of faith.

The dissection of the book into its proposed sources and contexts of expression has contributed to our understanding of the book as it came into being. But of equal importance, at least, is the book of Exodus in the only form about which we can be absolutely certain, the form in which we have received it as one part of the text of the Bible. The assembled book has an integrity all its own, different from the sources upon which it is dependent. It sets forth a message and an emphasis that none of those sources, insofar as we can recover them, can be seen to have presented. That message and that emphasis are theological. They confess the Presence of God and give the evidence for the confession, as well as its implications for Israel's life in faith.

The subject of this slim volume is this confession, in all the forms in which the book of Exodus presents it. I regard the book of Exodus as the book that gives the primary presentation of *the* theme of the Bible, the book, therefore, that influences the shape of the Bible as no other one book does, the book that may thus be considered, in a way, the beginning of the Bible. I have attempted in the chapters that follow to survey the book's presentation of this theme by summarizing and discussing as three separate blocks of material the three obvious layers of Exodus in its biblical form: a story layer, a requirement layer, and a layer concerned with making the story real and the requirements urgent to each new generation—a memory layer.

I have entitled these layers "sequences," both to suggest the single purpose of material we see in separate places in the canonical form of Exodus and also to emphasize that the layers, while separate in subject, are presentations of one theme. Each of the layers is dictated by, and is an expression of, the one theme, Presence of God, and each of them has been considered in the sequence of their logical development. Event precedes report (story), report becomes the basis of expectation (requirement), and repetition (memory) keeps both event and its report current and real.

In the presentation that follows, textual questions and problems of translation, source- and form-literary proposals, the reconstruction of historical circumstances, the comparative evaluation of commentary and monograph theory are omitted as outside the concern of this focused survey of the theme of Exodus and its varied expressions. These matters have been treated repeatedly and in detail elsewhere, by myself and by many others.[3] Whether any of these treatments are even minimally adequate remains to be demonstrated, probably in discussion with Moses, Joshua, and Aaron in some context of existence yet to come. I regard them all as important, as the Word Biblical Commentary *Exodus* will show, but they are outside the purview of the present survey of themes.

The story sequence of the book of Exodus, as the primary and narrative presentation of its theme, has been considered first. That story, the story of God's Presence with his people Israel, is related in Exodus 1:8–6:13; 6:28–11:10; 12:21–50; 13:17–14:31; 15:19–18:12; 19:1–20:21; 24:1–18; 32:1–34:9, 29–35; 40:34–38. In the canonical form of the book of Exodus, this story has been pulled apart at appropriate points to allow the insertion of material having to do with requirements posed by the reality of God's Presence and with the remembrance of that reality to the generations beyond the story, those for whom the past must become present if a requirement is to be taken seriously. The inserted passages of requirement—18:13-27; 20:1-17; 20:22-23:33; 34:10-28—have been considered the second sequence, and the inserted passages of remembrance—1:1-7; 6:14-27; 12:1-20; 13:1-16; 15:1-18; 25:1-31:18; 35:1-40:33—have been considered the third sequence, though the requirement and remembrance sequences often blend in reciprocal concern.

Thus I have attempted to deal with the theme of the book of Exodus, and the themes that theme has stimulated in a quite thematic way, with *the* theme and its subthemes dictating the sequence of treatment. This is not a theory of the sequence of composition of the book of Exodus, though it may suggest hints in such a direction. It is rather an attempt to take *the* theme and its subthemes as they are, in a narrative with defining addenda that have been a guidance to a great many believers across at least two dozen centuries. I confess at the onset that I am one of them, and I find great honor in belonging to a process of belief at the beginning of which stands the towering but stammering figure of Moses, son of the Levite Amram and his wife Jochebed.

2

THE SEQUENCE OF STORY

The place of story in human experience has yet to be appreciated adequately, except by young children, for whom the nourishing connection between imagination and experience remains unbroken. The young, of whatever chronological age, accept imagination and reality as one. The word *fantasy* is a grown-up invention designed to cover the embarrassment produced by a loss of the gift for dreaming. And the use of "story" as a euphemism for "lie" is a serious adult miscalculation, not least since one of the more eager requests children make of adults is, "Tell me a story."

Story is important to each of us, and at every level of our existence. We each have a story, and a thick cord of a story made up of many stories. What and who we are at any given point in the time-line of our living is an amalgam of event, influence, and response; and our recollection and recounting of that amalgam is a story that is part fact, part perception, and all truth. Event is followed immediately by memory. Thus is begun a process of selection that preserves, in accord with a complex variety of influences, only what is of first importance to the one who remembers and reports the remembrance.

When this process of recounting moves from an individual to a community level, the major difference in the process is the function of many memories and the addition of more controlling influences. And the end of the process, insofar as it ever has an end, is in this case both more universal and more refined. The Bible is a product of such a process, and the initial event and memory at its foundation is the event and memory of the Exodus.

Northrop Frye has made the provocative suggestion that "as the Exodus is the definitive deliverance and the type of all the rest [of "the rises and restorations"], we may say that mythically the Exodus is the only thing that really happens in the Old Testament."[1] While such a statement may seem at first to be an excessive oversimplification, I would suggest that we may go beyond it, as Frye proceeds to do,[2] though he follows a somewhat different path.

The Exodus is not "the only thing that really happens in the Old Testament," even in mythopoeic terms—but it *is* the event which, along with its recollection and recounting, shapes not just the Old Testament but the entire Bible. While this point has been accepted along thematic lines, and in reference to specific biblical books for some time,[3] it is now being given broader application along literary, theological, and even sociological lines.[4]

The story retold in the narrative sequence of the book of Exodus is not only a real story, it is my story as a Christian, and the "my story" of Jews and, in a very different way, the "my story" of oppressed and yearning people of many times and in many places.[5] Its reach into our lives is guaranteed first of all by our own deep need: We want the God who came then to come now, and we need the Presence that settled amongst Israel at Sinai to settle amongst us now. There is a sensation that somehow we are reading autobiography when we read the Exodus story believingly, a feeling of *déjà vu*, an aura of expectancy. The barriers of time and distance fall away, and we are somehow *there*, or there is somehow *here*, because the story of God's coming and the response of the sons (and daughters) of Israel is not only the story of the Bible—it is the story of every human being.

Think then, as you read the following summary of the sequence of story in the book of Exodus, that you are reading a diary you once kept, or that you are hearing a remembrance of your own pilgrimage of struggle from oppression to freedom. Each one of us has an Egypt, a wilderness, and a promised land; and each one of us is on a journey from the fragmentation of our own special enslavements to the wholeness of the place where we can be absolutely free, in God's Presence. We do not have to travel to the Nile Delta or to the Sinai Desert to be in those places of the soul, and we are not bound in our own story by the constraints of any time. The sequence of story in the book of Exodus is permeated with what Harold Bloom has called "the uncanny,"[6] the reach from the past that burns like a laser through the layers of repression and pretense and self-assurance to pull us up short, to confront us with the reality that is timeless because it is the single, ultimate reality of human existence: God.

It is by no means fortuitous that God is revealed in the story of Exodus as YHWH, "the *One* Who Always Is."[7] It is a logically sequential emphasis that reminds Israel at the far end of the Old Testament story, in a program for the revival of the covenant-faith that returned to the story of the Exodus, "Hear, Israel: YHWH is our God, YHWH [who is] *One*" (Deut 6:4). Is it any wonder that Jesus, according to the Gospel of Mark (12:29), should begin his recitation of the first of all the commandments with this confession, or that the first theologian of the Christian faith should write rapturously to the Church at Ephesus of "*one* body and *one*

Spirit, . . . one hope . . . , one Lord, one faith, one baptism, one God and Father of us all, the one before all and
through all and in all" (Eph 4:4-6).

As our God is One, so also our story is one. Whatever its
forms, its images, its details of time and place, its language
and its syntax, its simplicity or its sophistication, its breadth
or its limitation of exposure, its familiarity or its exclusivity,
our story is one story. And finally, it has but two characters.
Ultimately, it will have but One.

God keeping his promise

The beginning of the sequence of story in the book of
Exodus is determined in one way by the ending of the sequence of story in the book of Genesis. There the family
who by God's own covenant-promise belongs in the fair and
fecund land of Canaan is instead, if by reason of necessity, in
the delta land of Egypt. They have come there from hunger,
and they have found a hospitable sanctuary in a context of
favorable disposition.

They do not belong there, however, and the very first
sentence of the Exodus story gives us notice of the movement of the winds of change. A new Pharaoh has come to
the seat of power, and while our interest is fixed on the
identity of this unnamed king, the interest of the narrator
of the story is fixed on a far more crucial point: This leader
has no experience of Joseph and thus no disposition of
favor toward Joseph's family. That family, we have been
reminded by the first sequence of memory in the book of
Exodus (1:1-7, see pp. 100-102), has been growing rapidly
from its beginning in Jacob's twelve sons—so rapidly, in
fact, that they have become "a teeming swarm." That very
language is normally used to refer to great shoals of fish
(Gen 1:21; Ezek 47:9), infestations of small rodents and
reptiles (Lev 11:29-30), and even the flood of frogs that

inundates the Pharaoh, his court, and his country in the second of the proving mighty acts (Exod 8:1-15).

The first sequence of memory thus provides a bridge full of prospect, from the promise of God to the Fathers in faith to the fulfillment of that promise in the destiny of their descendants. These are the called-out Fathers, and their descendants are the election family, and their story is the beginning of the salvation history, the account of God's making a way back for the human family in rebellion. God's promise to the Fathers was twofold: a numberless progeny and an expansive land (Gen 12:1-2; 15:5, 18-21; 17:3-8). Exodus 1:1-7 leans backward toward the first part of that promise by naming the twelve fathers who represent the foundation of its fulfillment and by reporting the amazing proliferation of their offspring. We are thus prepared for the necessary next step, the provision of the land God has promised. As always (see pp. 97-100), the sequence of memory has a theological purpose—a point we must not allow our concern for demography or historical identification to obscure.

Thus are we reminded, at the very outset of the Exodus story, that what is happening in the Egyptian Delta is of God. The listing of Jacob's sons, the report of the rapid growth of their families, the allusion to the former favor Joseph enjoyed—all these describe the unfolding process of election, and prepare us for the story to come. God is placed at the center of events in Egypt indirectly, without being mentioned even once. And the grand schemes of the Pharaoh of Egypt to control and to limit this people of Israel are known to us for what they are: a futile waste of energy and time. It is a beginning like the beginning of Genesis 22 or the book of Job or the Passion narratives of the Gospels: we know how the terrible story will come out, and thus it holds for us no horror, only hope.

This hope is enhanced by the remarkable tension of the blessing of God's multiplication of Israel (the positive fulfillment of part one of his covenant-promise) with the awful oppression this blessing provokes. This positive, without the constraint of Joseph's high position, contributes to a horrendous negative. The more numerous Israel becomes, the nearer they are to the fulfillment of the second part of God's covenant-promise—but the more numerous they become, the greater is the new Pharaoh's fear of them as a threat, and the more draconian, therefore, are his measures of control and containment.

There is a subtle psychology at work in this narrative: the good which God does for Israel increases the harm attempted toward them by Pharaoh. The dramatic multiplication of their number brings closer the time when they will be able to manage and defend a land all their own; but it also makes their Egyptian neighbors ever more fearful of them and thus ever less hospitable toward them. The rapid expansion of their number makes their need of their own place more and more urgent, but it also seems to make their going to such a place less and less possible as the Pharaoh piles restriction onto requirement.

Of course this tension is not coincidence—it is a narrative *in medias res*, into which we are drawn by both empathy *and* theology. Though God is mentioned in the book of Exodus for the first time in its seventeenth verse, and then only in connection with the reverence of the midwives, his Presence is implicit from the opening, "And these are the names" of 1:1. He is the determinant force behind all that is taking place, including the increasing recalcitrance of the Pharaoh himself. We are in the hands of a brilliant theologian who is also a master storyteller. He has woven the traditions available to him into a fabric so engaging that it virtually makes his points by induction. Even the names he gives us are all laden with meaning, from Reuben, "Behold, a son!" to Joseph, "Increasing One." Even "Fair One" and "Fragrant One," the two believing and therefore blessed midwives, are a part of the cumulative lesson, which is declared between the lines: "God is, here." The electing, calling God of the Fathers has not relaxed his attention upon his people, not even for a moment.

Thus while the Pharaoh is attempting to wear the Israelites down, body and spirit, by unremitting hard labor, and to bring into check their high rate of healthy births by genocide, at first in secret and then as public policy, the God who Is, and who is here, is at work to set into motion step one of the fulfillment of the second half of his covenant-promise.

Coincident with these events, a man of the family of Levi had taken to wife a young woman who was also Levite. The wife became pregnant and gave birth to a son. (2:1-2)

This son, who is given the Egyptian name Moses, "boy-child," the Hebrew *yeled* or our own English "lad" or "kid," is the beginning of God's move to bring Israel to himself and to the land he promised to their Fathers, Abraham, Isaac, and Jacob. By a wonderfully witty piece of table-turning, this Hebrew boy-child thrown into the Nile as the Pharaoh has commanded, protected by the provision of a waterproof container, is rescued by the daughter of the Pharaoh who desires him dead, the father of the next king of Egypt, for whom the boy-child, in manhood, will become a nemesis. Then, to add ridicule onto joke, the boy's own mother is put on the payroll of the Pharaoh as wet-nurse-in-residence!

It is as delicious a piece of wool-pulling as one might wish for, and there can be no doubt at all by whose design all these events transpire. From the narrative of the faith of the midwives (1:17-21) to the corporate cry of oppressed Israel when this Pharaoh dies (2:23-25), there is no direct mention of God in this narrative; but we never once can have even the slightest doubt about the reality of his electing Presence.

By the engaging compactness of biblical narrative, Moses is taken from infancy to manhood. We are given no relief by digression. The account is moved steadily and suspensefully forward, without one wasted word. Moses' fatal blow against an Egyptian abusing a Hebrew reveals that he has not been compromised by his adoptive Egyptian family. But the result of this action is that he is ostracized by both his adoptive nation and by his biological family. To the Egyptians, he has become a murderous criminal. To the Israelites, he has become a liability, bringing them small advantage but tremendous risk.

He is left with little choice, and his flight to Midian shows that his mother has given him more than milk: Midian is where the other branch of the family, the Hagar-Ishmael-Keturah-Esau descendancy, is known to have a nomadic residence (see pp. 51–53). Midian is for Moses a strange new land, but also an old familiar land. The other side of the family of his Fathers is there. But much more important, the God of his Father *is* there, and is worshiped there. Moses' arrival in Midian, and his surprising reception there, are further evidence of the providence of the calling, electing God.

This point is made dramatically by what happens next, and by Moses' own summary interpretation of these events. He meets the seven daughters of a priest of Midian whose name is "Companion of God," and who is a priest who worships YHWH (Exod 18:10–11). Moses defends these girls against the bullying herdsmen who habitually delay their watering of their father's flock, thus endearing himself to these sisters, to one of them particularly, and to their father. In another flash of compact narrative, Moses settles down with the Midianite priest and becomes a husband and then a father. Following this event, Moses offers his understanding of all that has happened to him. He names his new son "Stranger There," explaining, "a stranger have I been in a land foreign to me" (Exod 2:22).

Moses, belonging neither to the Egyptians in Egypt nor to his own people in oppressive bondage there, has come at last to a place of belonging. He has a wife in Midian, a son, sisters-in-law, and a father-in-law, at least. For the first time in his life, he has a home. In Egypt, he was a sojourner, a tourist, a foreigner. In Midian, he is a resident, a native son, one member of an accepting family. And we are struck by the steady unfolding of God's providential arrangements for the people of his purpose.

But Moses' people in Egypt are still strangers in a land that is foreign to them. Their fathers, and his, went there for a temporary stay in the time of Joseph. As his stay there has come to an end, so must theirs. And, deftly, that is the direction which this brilliant narrative now takes.

"Now while these many days were passing," says the storyteller, yet another point of turning was reached, and passed, in Egypt. The Pharaoh of Moses' birth, early manhood, and criminal flight died. As has always been the case, in every nation ruled by power, this death meant transition, and those whose lot was bad hoped for some change for the better. For the very first time in the sequence of story in Exodus, the sons of Israel cry out for help to God (2:23), hoping for some relief, some slight improvement of their difficult circumstances. This is graphically suggested in this summary verse by the use twice of the word *ᵃvodah*, "agonized labor," by the verb and the noun for "groaning," and by two separate verbs for "cry out in need."

"And so of course God heard"—he always hears the earnest cry of his people if it is honest—and hearing, he remembered the covenant-promise to the Fathers, who are named, to make unmistakably clear what is now to take place. The sequence of story is begun with a report of change, a change that makes the fulfillment of the first part of God's covenant-promise more a liability than an asset. And so this prologue to its main sequence is ended with a report of yet another change, one that is to make their life in Egypt harder still.

Similarly, the first sequence of memory begins the book of Exodus with a listing of "the names of the sons of Israel," a looking back to the covenant-promise and a looking forward to its fulfillment. And it is echoed at both the beginning of the prologue to the sequence of story ("the people of the sons of Israel," the Pharaoh calls them, 1:9) and here at its conclusion ("the sons of Israel," 2:23, and the "covenant with Abraham, with Isaac, and with Jacob," 2:24).

The whole thrust of this introductory prologue to the sequence of story, then, is God keeping his promise to his election-people—to Abraham, Isaac, and Jacob, to Jacob's twelve sons, and now to the rapidly multiplying families of these sons. The first part of the promise has come to sufficient fulfillment to require the beginning of the fulfillment of the second part. God has remembered. Indeed, he has never forgotten. What he has done in the past guarantees what he will do in the future. The plight of the present is to be short-lived. God knows the suffering of Israel, "by experience" (2:25), and he has already been at work for them, long before their cry for help.

God revealing his Presence

The hero of the sequence of story in the book of Exodus, as indeed in the book of Exodus as a whole, is God. As we have seen, though God is mentioned at only two points in the first two chapters (and at that in but six of the forty-seven verses making up those two chapters) his promise and therefore his activity are implicit in every line of that prologue. The story moves next to God's revelation of his Presence to Moses, a sudden and dramatic announcement that he has been at hand all along. It is as if Moses turns a corner in the desolate wilderness of Sinai and finds God awaiting him there. The surprise, from the reader's point of view, is that Moses was surprised. But then those of us who could be expected most of all to know are often the ones who are most of all surprised by God's self-revelation.

This narrative has frequently been called the account of the call of Moses. Obviously, it includes the report of that call experience, but this is a narrative about God, not Moses. Moses here is the representative recipient of God's self-revelation. His call experience is a response to this revelation of God's Presence. Even his protests at his call are a carefully framed opportunity for us to be told more about God's adequacy than about Moses' inadequacies. Moses is a medium of the message of the revelation, but he is by no means the sole object of it. So also is Israel to be, at the climax of the story sequence of Exodus, a medium of a message of revelation. God's revelation of his Presence *begins* with Moses and with Israel; but it does not in any sense *end* with them.

Thus does every feature of the story drive toward a single purpose, the purpose of establishing that God is, and *is* here. Everything superfluous to that purpose has either been omitted or in some way bent toward its service.

This concentration of the sequence of story in Exodus is obvious as long as the narrative is read or heard as a whole, as it was intended to be. The biblical scholarship of the century following 1875, invaluable though many of its contributions certainly are, has trained our eyes to look too much on the supposed pieces of the narratives of the Bible and not enough on the narratives as a whole. We have too often treated the sequences of story in the Bible in a way which would seem to us utterly absurd were we to try it on the sequences of story of Dickens or Tolstoy or Hugo or Mann. We must not neglect what Robert Alter has called the "composite artistry" of the biblical narratives[8] if we are to understand the real subject and purpose of these stories.

Of no sequence of story in the Old Testament is this more true than it is of the sequence of the story of God's self-revelation in Exodus.

Deep in the wilderness around Mount Horeb ("Desolate Waste"), while attending his family's flock, Moses experiences a theophany. It is important that we keep in mind that this report follows immediately upon the statement that God has heard the multiplied cries of Israel in Egypt, has seen them, and knows by experience their suffering. His purpose in Israel has been under way since Abraham. His promise to Abraham and his election of Abraham's descendancy is coming rapidly to fulfillment. Within the crucible of Israel's oppression, he has molded a deliverer, and even as their cry for help comes to a crescendo, God reveals both his Presence and his intention to Moses.

The flaming thornbush that attracts Moses' attention is of course a theophanic symbol. The storyteller describes it as the appearance of a *mal'akh*, "the messenger of YHWH in a blaze of fire from the middle of a thornbush." What Moses sees is the form, apparently, of the thornbush, for what draws him toward this sight is the fact that despite the fire, the thornbush retains its form: "the thornbush, enveloped in the flame, was still the thornbush—none of it was destroyed!" This strange fire is the fire of guidance in the wilderness (Exod 13:21-22), the fire of Sinai (Exod 19:18; Deut 4:12, 15, 33), the fire of the flaming sword constantly turning in every direction and guarding the way to the tree of life (Gen 3:24). Northrop Frye has called it "the fire of life,"[9] and Samuel Terrien has described it as "a symbol of prompt becoming," that "does not consume its own fuel and survives its own death" and "suggests the slow and sustained becoming of historical transformation."[10]

As poetic as these elegant and somewhat abstract descriptions are, the Exodus narrative is far more direct: The thornbush all aflame but unconsumed is the visible symbol

of the Presence of God, an "unusual sight" that attracts
Moses' attention. Once he approaches the bush for a closer
look, the sight of a symbol is displaced by the sound of
God's voice.

As always in the Old Testament, the visual dimension of
the Presence of God is deemphasized, and the audible dimension is given primacy. The self-revelation of God is deliberately non-iconic, deliberately conceptual, and focused on
specific, action-oriented event. This is precisely the reason
why all accounts of God's appearances throughout the Old
Testament are only vaguely visual, involving obviously ever-
changeable forms such as fire (as here) or cloud (Exod 14:19–
20; Isa 6:1–4) or man-messenger-God (as in Gen 18 and 19)
or "something like a mosaic pavement of *lapis lazuli*, like the
span of the heavens in depth" (Exod 24:10) or all God's
"goodness" passing by (Exod 33:18–34:9). Here, as in every
other case in the Old Testament, the word almost immediately eclipses the image, which functions almost solely as an
attention-getter.

Thus before Moses can look closely at the thornbush, he
hears a voice calling his name. He responds and learns that
he is on holy ground and hearing the voice of the God of his
father (3:6), who is the God also of the three great Fathers in
faith, Abraham, Isaac, and Jacob. That voice is the subject of
this story, not the fire and not Moses. And the announcement the voice makes is the one which the beginning of
the Exodus sequence of story has prepared us to expect:
YHWH, fully aware of his covenant-promise to the Fathers
and of the difficult plight of Israel in Egypt, is now about to
set into motion the fulfillment of the second part of his
promise. He is bringing the multiplying progeny out of
Egypt and into the land he has in mind for them, "a good
and roomy land, a land gushing with milk and honey" (3:8),
where they can fulfill the purpose of their election.

Moses further learns that he is to be the one sent, the

chosen deliverer who is to lead Israel forth from Pharaoh's tight grip. This revelation draws from Moses a protest of inadequacy, and this protest is the storyteller's brilliant springboard into the heart of his narrative. Moses' inadequacy is real. His protest is no exaggeration. God himself does not deny his frightened "Who am I, that I am to go along to Pharaoh, that I am to bring the sons of Israel forth out of Egypt?" (3:11) It is by no means *Moses* who is qualified to deliver Israel from the Pharaoh's bondage. God has never once had such an option in view. As the subsequent narrative repeatedly shows, what is to be done, in Egypt and beyond it, can only be done by God himself. That is the point of the revelation on Horeb, and of the announcement that God is beginning the deliverance phase of his work of election for and with Israel. At the very outset of this process, God establishes who and how *he* is. Who and how Moses is is entirely secondary.

To Moses' thrice-repeated emphatic *I*, God replies instantly, "The point is, *I AM* with you" (3:12). Moses has the wrong *I* emphasized. How like us, whenever we are faced with a challenge, to think first of ourselves and the resources we lack. The teller of the sequence of story in Exodus knows his reader because he knows himself, and knows himself because he knows God. And by this brilliant turn of the narrative of Horeb, he pulls us, in sympathy, into Moses' position, and so prepares us for the real lesson he wants and needs to teach. "I AM with you," says God, the real hero and center of this entire account. This declaration appropriately shifts our attention, along with that of Moses, to the real issue: It is *God* who has elected Moses, and us, and it is not what Moses, or we ourselves, can and cannot do that is important, it is what *God* can do. To that question, Moses turns immediately, and the way is opened for the single most important revelation of the Bible, a revelation for which we are now prepared by God's emphatic I AM, *'ehyeh* in Hebrew.

"Suppose I *do* go to Israel in Egypt," Moses says, "and report that I am sent by the God of their fathers—they may well say 'So what?' What then am I to say to them?" (3:13)

Moses' use of the title "the God of your fathers," an echo of the title given to him by the voice from the thornbush in Exodus 3:6, makes clear that the question he anticipates from Israel, no doubt the very question rising in his own mind, has little to do with identity and much to do with authority. Though the literal translation of the question posed by Moses is, "What is his name?" the meaning of the question must be understood in the light of Moses' protest of 3:11 and God's response to it. It must be understood in the light of the broader significance of the Hebrew word *shem*, "name," and of the answer God gives in 3:14. *Shem* in reference to God is (like the nouns *kabod*, "glory," and *panim*, "face") a reference to God's Presence. The Oxford Hebrew Lexicon defines *shem* as the equivalent of "reputation" and as an embodiment of "the (revealed) character" of YHWH.[11] God's answer to Moses' question is a description of his "revealed character," an assertion of his eternal being, a claim of authority, and a summary of his self-revelation. By no means is this answer a name. In effect, Moses asks God, "Just what are You able to do?"

Thus is God's answer unmistakably clear, taken quite literally, and without any of the emendation, ingenious substitution, or imaginative imposition that have frequently been heaped upon it. "*'Ehyeh 'asher 'ehyeh*," God says, "I AM the One Who Always Is." This response is anticipated by God's emphatic "I AM" in 3:12 and echoed by his statement to Moses for Israel at the end of 3:14, "I AM has sent me forth to you." More literally still, the answer of 3:14 is "I AM that I AM," or even "I AM always I AM." *'Ehyeh* occurs once in 3:12, and three times in 3:14, and becomes the basis for the revelation of the tetragram YHWH, a name generally transliterated "Yahweh," in 3:15.

D. J. McCarthy refers to "the spell of repetition" cast by these four "I AMs"[12] and J. P. Fokkelman notes that the explanation of the name is given before the name itself is given.[13] Northrop Frye suggests, "we might come closer to what is meant in the Bible by the word 'God' if we understood it as a verb, and not a verb of simple asserted existence but a verb implying a process accomplishing itself."[14] The late Roland de Vaux has proposed that "I AM that I AM" is equivalent to "I am Yahweh" ("ʾⁱni YHWH"),[15] the self-confessional, self-revealing phrase that occurs so frequently in the Old Testament in a varied series of forms.

The play of these words based on the verb *hayah*, "to be," obscured in English translation, is obvious in Hebrew:

hayah	"to be"
ʾehyeh	"I am"
yihyeh	"he is"
Yahweh	"The One Who Always Is"
ʾehyeh ʾᵃsher ʾehyeh	"I am that I am"

The usual personal pronoun plus a participle is replaced by

ʾᵃni Yahweh   "I (am) the One Who Always Is"

The *ʾᵃni*, "I," functions as *ʾehyeh*, "I am," and Yahweh, "the One Who Always Is" functions as a participial form of the irregular verb *hayah*, "to be." This phrase, then, is further compacted to "I (am) He," equal to "I (am) the One," as in these powerful confessions in Deutero-Isaiah:

"I (am) the One Who Always Is, no other is—
    Molder of right, Creator of dark,

24   EXODUS

Maker of wholeness, Creator of 'wrong'—
I (am) the One Who Always Is,
    Maker of all these things."

                                    (Isa 45:6–7)

"I (am) first and I (am) last
    —apart from me, there is no God."

                                    (Isa 44:6)

"I, I (am) He,
    Canceler of your rebellions for my own good
    —your sins I just won't think about."

                                    (Isa 43:25)

In each of these references, as in the 6,823 occurrences
of YHWH in the Old Testament, the special meaning of
the unique name is at least implicit; often it is explicit.[16]
This tetragram is, in a way, God's foundational and ultimate self-revelation in the Old Testament. Thus the significance of Exodus 3:14–17, the only passage in the Old
Testament in which God himself is represented giving the
explanation of his own special name, cannot be overstated.
In a way, these verses are a compact summary of the entire
sequence of story in the book of Exodus—God is; really,
he *is*. Without beginning, without ending, before any beginning and beyond any ending we can imagine, an eternal
Presence, eternally in the present tense, always both here
and there, never once leaving his people (which is to say
the human family entire) not even for an instant, the One
Who Always Is.

What remains is that this eternal, never-absent Presence
be demonstrated and proven beyond any doubting, first to
Moses, then to Israel, and then to Pharaoh, his government,
and the people of Egypt.

Having connected his name Yahweh with the title, "the
God of the Fathers . . . Abraham . . . Isaac . . . Jacob"

(3:15, but also 3:6, 13, 16), the One Who Always Is proceeds to anticipate that proof by predicting as impending the Exodus from Egypt, the fulfillment of the covenant-promise of land, and the necessary coercion of the Pharaoh and his nation to this intention. In a dramatic preview of what is to come, and in a repetition of the motif of 3:11-12, that it is he alone who will be able to bring these predictions to fulfillment, Yahweh declares emphatically ("Now I know very well," 3:19) that no power save his can induce the Pharaoh to release Israel. Yahweh therefore will stretch forth *his* hand, and far from being merely cooperative, the Pharaoh will *drive* Israel from the Delta, and the Egyptians will load them down with expensive gifts as they go. In this promise, the sequence of story through what is now Exodus 13 is briefly summed up, and the narrator turns immediately to the first step in Yahweh's demonstration of his eternally present Being, the persuasion of Moses, his deliverer.

The three signs given to Moses as symbols to Israel and to Egypt of the authority with which he comes to them from Yahweh have a triple function in the sequence of story.

The first function of these signs is the one made obvious by Moses' concern about his own credibility: "Look here, they won't trust me, and they won't pay attention to my report" (4:1).

The second function of the signs is Moses' concern about *Yahweh's* credibility, a concern that permeates this narrative from 3:13 through 4:17. It is *Yahweh* in whom Moses and Israel and the Egyptians must believe if the Exodus is to take place. Moses is but a messenger, the one who is to announce and then interpret a series of staggering events.

There is yet, however, a third function of the signs; it is the most important if least obvious: its target is those not a part of the historical Exodus who have yet to be convinced and so to come to belief. The signs are the first hint of the proof of Yahweh's Presence, the anticipation of the sequence of extraordinary events by which the generations yet to come, ourselves included, can become a part of the theological Exodus, the Exodus in faith, the ongoing Exodus, the never-ending opportunity for Exodus. We, too, are elected as recipients of the self-revelation, as channels of election, as a people in a movement of Exodus.

At the same time, the three signs, along with the questions that call them forth, present us with a tension of doubt and belief. On the one hand, Moses and Israel yearn for the freedom they think they cannot have, hoping for a relationship they believe will be denied them. On the other hand, Yahweh acts to establish the truth of his claim of Being, to demonstrate the reality of his Presence. It is a tension between whose polarities we ourselves vacillate, so in this additional way this ancient story is *our* story.

The signs of the staff which became a serpent and of the Nile water changed to blood on the dry earth (the first demonstrated, the second only predicted here) are of course performed by the Yahweh-Moses partnership in Egypt. The sign of the skin-diseased hand is not repeated in Egypt, though a much more severe infection of skin disease afflicts Miriam in the Sinai-to-Paran wilderness (Num 12), as a result of her rebellion against the authority of Moses. If there was an original narrative of Moses' employing this sign in Egypt, it may have been omitted in the final sequence of story in the book of Exodus because of the negative implications of this infectious skin disease.[17]

Moses' further resistance even after Yahweh's demonstration of two signs and the prediction of a third is a dramatic indication of the tension between trust and doubt, confidence and lack of confidence, obedience and rebellion throughout the sequence of story in Exodus. Yahweh's understandably irritated response includes yet another emphasis of his claim of Being: his twice-repeated and doubly emphatic assertion, "I AM with your mouth." Moses at last capitulated ("Pardon, Lord: please send anybody you want to send," 4:13), and Aaron is introduced as Moses' spokesperson, just as Moses is himself Yahweh's spokesperson. Once more, it is made unquestionably clear to us that the Presence and the power that will count in Egypt, as anywhere else, is Yahweh's, and that what Yahweh will do there is an additional dimension of his self-revelation.

So Moses sets off for Egypt, with Jethro's blessing (4:18), and with the further assurance of Yahweh that Moses is empowered to do the wondrous deeds he has just witnessed. Yahweh also announces his plan to make the Pharaoh's mind obstinate as a means of proving beyond any cavil, Israelite or Egyptian, that he is both present and in control. In the Yahweh-Moses partnership, Moses is to deliver the announcements and the warnings, then put into motion the signs Yahweh has empowered. Yahweh will prevent the Pharaoh from being convinced prematurely, from coming around too soon, before the events and causes that prompt the Exodus are known to have only one possible explanation: the powerful Presence of Yahweh in Egypt, and with his people Israel.

By allusion to what is now the tenth of the mighty acts with which Yahweh intends to prove his Presence, the contrast between the power of Yahweh and that of the divine representative of Egypt's gods, the Pharaoh, is made. Yahweh declares that his son, his firstborn, Israel, must be permitted to leave Egypt to worship him, warning Pharaoh, with a pointedly parallel phrase, that "your son, your firstborn," will otherwise be killed. It is the announcement of how things are to be, the preview of the conclusion to the proof of the Presence acts, and also the reason for that conclusion. Many times over in the sequence of story through Exodus 15, this declaration is remade.

The strange narrative of Yahweh's fearful encounter with Moses during the journey from Midian to Egypt has apparently been included in the sequence of story at this point as a means of assurance. Moses, like all the rest of the Israelites of the Exodus and the wilderness wandering, could not be permitted to bypass the important symbol-in-the-flesh of the covenant commitment. Born in Egypt and reared in Pharaoh's household, Moses could be assumed to have had at most only the partial circumcision of the Egyptians, a "disgrace" according to Joshua 5:9. Thus at the beginning of his work as Yahweh's deliverer, Moses had to be properly circumcised, just as the new generation born in the wilderness had to be circumcised, even though they were adults. By this act, the "disgrace" of their neglect was rolled away, and the place where this occurred came to be called Gilgal, "roll-away" (Josh 5:2–9).

The paragraph is a difficult one, not least because of the ambiguity of its pronouns and its apparent reference to half-obscure practices connected apparently with both puberty and marriage. As the sequence of story now stands, however, this passage provides a dramatic, if somewhat startling, conclusion to Yahweh's revelation of his Presence and the difference that Presence demands. It is followed only by brief notices of Moses' rendezvous with Aaron and their arrival and favorable reception by Israel in Egypt.

God proving his Presence

Despite the positive reception given initially by Israel to Moses and Aaron, and to their announcement of Yahweh's impending rescue (4:29–31), the first approach to Pharaoh ends disastrously. Not only is their request for Israel's release for a pilgrimage to Yahweh turned down—it is put down as absurd and as an indication that Israel does not have sufficient work to keep them busy. The outcome of what was to be the first step to freedom is thus a quick-march deeper into oppressive slave labor. The people of Israel are to meet, without reduction, the quotas of bricks expected of them *and* gather the chopped straw heretofore supplied them by their Egyptian masters. When these quotas are not met, the Israelite section leaders are whipped by their Egyptian bosses. This, in turn, leads them to protest their treatment to Pharaoh himself, who gives them the reason for their new hardship:

> "*Lazy* is what you are, *lazy* you are indeed, saying, 'Let us go; let us offer sacrifice to Yahweh.' Now go get to work! Straw will not be provided you, and you will produce the full measure of bricks!" (5:17–18).

Thus do the section leaders turn on Moses and Aaron, and thus does Moses turn on Yahweh: "Why have you sent me here for *this?*" (5:22) In view of the high promise connected with Yahweh's revelation of himself on Horeb/Sinai, the question seems a reasonable one. The negative response of Pharaoh and the acceleration of hardship for Israel amount to an apparent cancellation of Yahweh's claims of Presence and power. Indeed, the Pharaoh arrogantly pleads ignorance of any Yahweh and indifference therefore to his commands and to the requests of his people Israel. And, as the Pharaoh cancels all Moses' plans with apparent impunity, even Moses' confidence in Yahweh is undermined. Can Yahweh really save his elect people from further Egyptian oppression? Has not their situation deteriorated rather than improved? Has Yahweh's self-revelation been misunderstood, or misleading, or has it come to a sudden, defeated halt?

This pattern of divine promise apparently negated is a didactic device that recurs in biblical narrative. Here as elsewhere[18] it provides a dramatic focus for what actually happens by giving the appearance that what God has promised is simply not possible. Pharaoh is thus allowed to set himself

up for a terrible fall—Yahweh even assists him in his fool-
hardy display of hubris. Almost without our realizing it, the
sequence of story has drawn us into a mighty contest, upon
whose outcome rests the ultimate fate of Israel, and thus of
Yahweh's own purpose of redemption for the human family.
The form of the narrative through the final escape of the
Exodus itself is set by this introductory account in 5:1-6:1,
as is the tension upon which the story is thrust forward.

Before the contest is continued, the sequence of story of
the book of Exodus is interrupted by an appropriate reminder of Israel's covenantal commitment from the time of
the Fathers: Abraham, Isaac, and Jacob. Beginning with a
fourfold repetition of the self-proclamatory statement,
"I am the One Who Always Is" (^{2a}ni YHWH, 6:2, 6-8), this
section specifies the continuing fulfillment of the
covenant-promise to the Fathers in the impending Exodus
from Egypt, justifies by genealogy the choice of first Aaron
then Moses as Yahweh's partners in the deliverance, and
moves into a preview of the proof-of-Presence chapters in
7:8-11:10, 12:21-50.

This inserted section, one of three lengthy blocks of material (6:2-7:7; 25:1-31:18; 35:1-40:33) setting forth priestly
and liturgical interests, is often regarded as an interruption
of the continuity of narrative of Exodus, in part a duplication of information given already and in part a supplement
to that information. A consideration of this section as a part
of the whole of the sequence of story of the book of Exodus,
however, rather than as a block of inserted material, gives it
a somewhat different appearance. What we have here, at the
most appropriate point in the sequence of story, precisely
when things are looking bad for Yahweh's promise and so
for Yahweh's people, is a reminder of the covenant-promise
to the Fathers, of the consequent election of Israel, and of
Yahweh's self-revelation of his event-bringing Presence to
Moses on Horeb.

In a way, Exodus 6:2–13 renews the very beginning of the book of Exodus, a part of the sequence of memory (see below, pp. 100–102) from the priestly circle. It also reemphasizes the essential dictum of faith presented to Moses on Horeb/Sinai and summed up in the special name YHWH, "The One Who Always Is." And it provides a justification, in another inserted sequence of memory, for the significant role of Aaron, the prototypical "chief" or "high" priest. Then it resumes the narrative sequence after these urgent reminders at the very point at which the movement toward Exodus runs into the brick wall of the Pharaoh's ignorance and self-congratulating arrogance.

The 6:2–7:7 passage is not, therefore, a duplicatory interruption of the sequence of story. It is rather a didactic aside *in medias res,* an essential lesson at a teachable moment of need, a reminder at a point of initial difficulty (before the far more difficult circumstances yet to come) of two essential realities: (1) the covenant-promise of Israel's election by Yahweh and (2) the Presence of Yahweh moving to fulfill that promise. What remains is the proof of that Presence, and that proof is made in the progress toward the fulfillment of the promise. As the sequence of story continues, heading into greater difficulties and more discouragements, we have been given a bright North Star by which to guide our course: it is *Yahweh* who has promised, and Yahweh *is,* here. Whatever happens in the moment, we must live according to the longer view faith affords us.

The gauntlet Pharaoh has thrown down in his arrogant ignorance, "who is Yahweh?" (5:2), is taken up by Moses and Aaron in their next reported audience with Pharaoh. They make "a wondrous deed" (7:9) to establish their authority and the credibility of their claims about Yahweh. This wondrous deed is a variation on the sign of the staff-become-a-serpent given first to Moses on Horeb (4:2–5) and then presumably to Israel in Egypt (4:30), a variation dramatically augmented.

Where Moses saw his staff transformed into a *nachash*, a "serpent" he clearly assumed to be dangerous, this same staff, now called "Aaron's staff," becomes in front of Pharaoh a *tannin*, a "monstrous snake" (7:10). *Nachash* is a generic term, the equivalent of the common use in American English of the word *snake*. *Tannin*, at least in most of its fifteen Old Testament occurrences (I suggest in *all* of them), refers to a reptile of horrendous proportions, such as the primordial sea monster. The connection of Pharaoh with this term (Ezekiel calls the Pharaoh a *tannin* in 29:3 and 32:2, and Deutero-Isaiah implies as much, Isaiah 51:9) underscores its use here.

Thus the "monstrous snake" which Moses' staff becomes before Pharaoh is a dramatic expansion of the sign of the staff, and a clear prediction of how things are going to turn out. The primordial sea monster is a plaything to Yahweh, so the Pharaoh of Egypt can hardly be more. When Yahweh changes Aaron's staff into a *tannin* (an allusion to the sea monster and a derisive nickname for Pharaoh) and the Pharaoh's "wise scholars and magicians" repeat "by their arcane arts" this same incredible transformation, "then, suddenly, Aaron's staff gobbled up all their staffs!" (7:12c). The use of "staff" instead of "monstrous snake" in this statement is a further reminder of the sign in progress as well as an announcement of Yahweh's superiority.

The statement that Pharaoh remained unconvinced by this double miracle is no surprise to us—we have been told already that such would be the case (3:19; 4:21–23). We have also been told already that Yahweh will rain upon Pharaoh and his Egypt "an array of extraordinary deeds," after which Pharaoh will be eager for an Exodus of Israel (3:20). To that array of proving deeds, the sequence of story now moves, and we know already what the outcome is going to be.

The language by which the extraordinary deeds are described as "plagues" is inappropriate, except perhaps from the perspective of the Egyptians, who suffer their effects. These deeds are Yahweh's proving actions, by which he demonstrates in progressive fashion the reality of his claim of Being and Presence, to Israel, to Egypt, and finally to Pharaoh's court and to Pharaoh himself. They are nothing less than actions of self-revelation on Yahweh's part.

Any attempt to explain these mighty acts as exaggerated natural phenomena is likewise inappropriate. They are specifically called "extraordinary deeds" (3:20), "great deeds of vindication" (6:6; 7:4), "signs and wondrous deeds" (7:3), "an act of a God" (by Pharaoh's learned men, 8:19), "my whole arsenal of blows" (by Yahweh, 9:14), and "stroke of judgment" (also by Yahweh, 11:1), and their specific intent is to demonstrate beyond any question Yahweh's incomparability (note 8:10 and 9:14). They are a means of theological statement, not a description of unusual natural history in the delta of Egypt, and they are presented in the sequence of story of Exodus as miracles. Whatever opinions we may have about the nature of the miraculous, the meaning of Yahweh's mighty acts for the sequence of story of Exodus will be seriously distorted if we attempt to rationalize their miraculous content.

We must also keep in mind the cumulative impact these "wondrous deeds" are intended to have, not only upon Israel and upon the Egyptians and Pharaoh, but also upon the successive hearers and readers of this sequence of story. We are given from the start of that sequence the confession the mighty acts are to demonstrate: Yahweh is, Yahweh *is* here, Yahweh is here keeping his promise of salvation to his covenant people. All who doubt that confession in any way are left, by the mighty acts, with no reason for further doubt. Even the last resister to belief, the Pharaoh himself, is able to hold out only because Yahweh, in order to make the proof completely obvious, prolongs Pharaoh's resolve not to give in. First Israel, then "the learned men" of Egypt, then the courtiers of Pharaoh and the Egyptian people come to belief. But the Pharaoh, because of Yahweh's firming of his resolve, holds out beyond all reason. The verses of the sequence of story depicting this resistance, seen all together, show the dramatic repetition of this important theme:

Anticipating the Resistance:

3:19: "Now I know very well that the king of Egypt will not give you permission to go. . . ."

4:21: "And I will make his mind obstinate, and he will not send out the people."

5:2: But Pharaoh replied, "Who is Yahweh, that I should pay attention to *his* voice, and so send out Israel? I have no knowledge of Yahweh, and *Israel,* I am not *about* to send out!"

7:3: "At the same time, *I* will make Pharaoh stubborn-minded, then pile up signs and wondrous deeds in the land of Egypt; Pharaoh will pay no attention to you. . . ."

The Resistance in Action:

7:13: But the mind of Pharaoh was unchanged. He paid no attention to them, just as Yahweh had predicted.

7:14: So Yahweh said to Moses, "The mind of Pharaoh is heavy and dull; he refuses to send out the people."

7:22-23: So Pharaoh's mind was again obstinate; he paid no attention to them, just as Yahweh had predicted. Pharaoh turned his back on them, entered his palace, and put the whole business out of his mind.

8:15: The minute Pharaoh saw that there was an end to the frogs, however, he steeled his mind and would pay no attention to them, just as Yahweh had predicted.

The Sequence of Story

8:19:	Then the learned men said to Pharaoh, "This is an act of a God." But Pharaoh's mind remained obstinate, and he would pay no attention to them, just as Yahweh had predicted.
8:32:	Once again, however, Pharaoh steeled his mind, this time as well, and he would not send out the people.
9:7:	Yet when Pharaoh sent out and saw that not even a single animal from the livestock of Israel had died, Pharaoh's mind remained heavy and dull, and he did *not* send out the people.
9:34-35:	Yet Pharaoh, seeing that the rain and the hail and the thunderclaps stopped, gave in once more to wrong-headedness, and so steeled his mind; he did, and the members of his court did. Thus Pharaoh's mind remained unchanged, and he did not send out the Israelites, as Yahweh had predicted through Moses.

Yahweh Reinforcing the Resistance:

9:12:	Yet Yahweh made obstinate the mind of Pharaoh, so he paid no attention to them, just as Yahweh had predicted to Moses.
9:16:	"In fact for this one reason alone will I cause you still to stand firm, to the end that I show you my strength, in result of which my name will be celebrated throughout the earth."
10:1-2:	Next, Yahweh said to Moses, "Go to Pharaoh— because *I* have made heavy and dull both his mind and the minds of the members of his court, to the end that I be taken seriously through these signs of mine right in their own territory, and to the end that you may recount again and again in the hearing of your son and your grandson that I amused myself aggravating the Egyptians, and that I set my signs against them in order that you may know by experience that I am Yahweh."
	Thus:

10:20:	Yahweh once more made Pharaoh's mind obstinate, however, and he did not send out the sons of Israel.
10:27:	At that very moment, Yahweh made Pharaoh's mind obstinate, and he did not consent to their going out.
11:9-10:	Then Yahweh said to Moses, "Pharaoh will pay no attention to you: my purpose is that my wondrous deeds may be many in the land of Egypt." So Moses and Aaron did all these wondrous deeds in Pharaoh's presence, and Yahweh made Pharaoh's heart obstinate, and he did not send out the sons of Israel from his land.

Even after the Pharaoh has at last been allowed by Yahweh to relent, following the devastation of the tenth mighty act, with its threat of termination for the Egyptian nation, Yahweh once again turns Pharaoh's mind. Though Israel has fled the delta with the eager consent of Pharaoh and his nation, Yahweh's proof of his Presence remains unfinished still:

14:4:	". . . I will make Pharaoh's mind obstinate; he will come chasing after them, and I will win myself glory over Pharaoh and all his force, so that the Egyptians will know by experience that I am Yahweh."
14:8:	Thus Yahweh made obstinate the mind of Pharaoh, king of Egypt, so that he chased after the sons of Israel. . . .
14:17-18:	". . . Just watch me making the Egyptians' minds obstinate, so that they will come after them, enabling me to win myself glory over Pharaoh and over all his infantry, over his chariotry and over his riders. Thus the Egyptians will know by experience that I am Yahweh, in my winning glory for myself over Pharaoh and over his chariotry and over his riders."

With this final forced resistance of Pharaoh, and the total defeat that follows it, the proof of Yahweh's Presence, to the Egyptians and to Israel, is both complete and effective. The Egyptians' force of "six hundred crack chariots" (14:6) was drowned in the onrush of the manipulated sea. And as for Israel, safe and dry on the Sinai side of the sea,

14:30–31:   Thus did Yahweh rescue Israel that day from the power of the Egyptians. Israel saw the Egyptians dead upon the edge of the sea, and Israel saw the great power that Yahweh unleashed against the Egyptians. So the people were in awe of Yahweh— and in consequence, they put their trust in Yahweh and in Moses, his servant.

The climactic celebration of this proof, and also, in its root form the oldest, is the victory hymn of Moses and Miriam in Exodus 15:1–21, often called "the Song of the Sea," and is treated more fully as a part of the sequence of memory (see below, pp. 108–12). In its present and obviously much expanded form, this hymn celebrates the proof of Yahweh's Presence in the victory over the Pharaoh and his forces at the Sea (15:1b–12, 21). Also it celebrates this proof in the guidance of Israel through the wilderness into the promised land, in the paralysis through fear of those who would deny Israel access to that land and those who would vie with Israel for its control and possession (15:13–16), and even in the fulfillment of the ancient covenant-promise in the establishment of Israel in that land with Yahweh dwelling amongst them and ruling "forever and without interruption" (15:17–18). The conclusion to the hymn, in fact, makes reference to the Temple built by Solomon on the hill of Zion, the "new Sinai," and to the Jerusalem theology of Yahweh's unending kingship from there (compare 15:17–18 with Psalms 47, 93, 96–99). The hymn is thus a summary of Yahweh's salvation of, and special provision for, his elect people Israel, across at least three centuries.

The nucleus of this hymn, however, is its dramatic statement of Yahweh's real and incomparable[19] Presence. Yahweh is called "might" and "song of Praise," "salvation," "God," and "God of my father," and "a warrior," and is described as the one who has thrown "Pharaoh's chariots and his whole force into the sea." Pharaoh indeed is depicted as an arrogant egomaniac buoyed by a groundless self-confidence:

"I will chase,
I will catch,
I will loot,
My battle lust will satisfy itself,
I will empty,
I will possess!"   (15:9)

And Yahweh is presented as one who has at his command the ancient primeval deep, and who has but to blow with his wind to send this proud king and all his force sinking down like lead into the collected waters (15:8, 10). The end of all this, the end also of the sequence of proving mighty acts is the recurring rhetorical question,

"Who is like you among the gods, Yahweh?
Who is like you,
          magnificent in holiness,
          awesome in praiseworthy deeds,
          doing the extraordinary?" (15:11)

This is what the mighty acts and Egypt are all about, the establishment beyond any question of the powerful, all-ruling, and saving Presence of Yahweh. It is a proof that is presented, with an inexorable and progressive rhythm, by the development of a rising series of parallel themes. The

first of these themes is the belief of Israel, superficially per-
suaded with ease (4:29–31) but just as easily lapsing again and
again into disbelief (5:20–21; 14:10–12).

The second of them is the belief of Pharaoh's "wise scholars and magicians," his advisers, his people, and ultimately
the Pharaoh himself. The third of them is the divinely
prompted *disbelief* of the Pharaoh, by which Yahweh's proof
of his Presence is carried beyond any conceivable need for
further demonstration. And the fourth of them, an invisible
but ever-present motif, is our own belief in Yahweh's acting
Presence, the belief of all who hear or read or in any other
way come to know this sequence of self-revelation.

Thus are the mighty acts presented as an accelerating
sequence of self-revelation, following the authenticating
prologue miracle of the rod and the monstrous snake (7:8–
13). The first of them, the changing of water from the river
Nile into blood (the extent of the transformation varied according to the source of the narrative), is immediately duplicated by "the learned men of Egypt" (7:14–25). Because of
this duplication, Pharaoh, who has already confessed his
total ignorance of Yahweh (5:1–2) is not even slightly im-
pressed, and therefore is convinced of nothing. The second
mighty act, the teeming multiplication of the frogs along the
Nile (8:1–5, also with a varied report), is also duplicated by
the "learned men," a tie of discomforting result, as it served
more to aggravate Pharaoh's problem than to provide him
with a victory. Once the frogs are killed by Yahweh, Pharaoh
remains indifferent both to the Hebrews and to their God
Yahweh.

With the third mighty act, there is the beginning of a
breakthrough. The learned men of Egypt are unable to turn
"the loose soil of the earth" into a swarm of gnats, and they
even advise Pharaoh that the blanket of gnats aggravating
Egypt is "an act of a God" (8:16–19). Still the Pharaoh does
not believe, despite the confession of his wonder-workers

that their power, though considerable, has been surpassed. So there follows the fourth mighty act, a devastating mixed swarm of flying insects which, according to the tradition preserved by Psalm 78:45, "ate on" the Egyptians (8:20–32). This time there is a second breakthrough: The Pharaoh is concerned enough by the effect of this annoyance to propose a concession, giving Moses permission to offer sacrifices in Egypt, and when that proves unacceptable, to take Israel into the nearby wilderness for such worship. He has even come to enough belief to request Moses to "pray in my behalf" (8:28e). When the insect swarm departs, however, he cancels the permission he has given, raising a question about his sincerity to start with.

The fifth mighty act, "a decimating epidemic" throughout the Egyptians' livestock (9:1–7), appears to have some effect on Pharaoh until he learns that the epidemic has not affected Israel's livestock. Perhaps he thinks the epidemic a curious and passing fluke, or perhaps he is too reluctant to risk losing the Israelite flocks and herds. Whatever the case, he will not permit Israel to depart Egypt. The sixth mighty act, an infection of inflamed swellings breaking into septic sores on humans and animals alike (9:8–12) produces the additional breakthrough of a total defeat of Egypt's learned men. They not only cannot duplicate the infection, but they are helpless to prevent it even in their own bodies. This time, for the first time, Yahweh's strengthening of Pharaoh's resistance implies that he is about to come to belief. With Yahweh's interference, however, that belief is of course impossible.

The seventh mighty act, a destructive and death-dealing hailstorm (9:13–35), reveals a further breakthrough: Some members of the court of Pharaoh, his closest advisers, have come to belief in Yahweh's word, and they heed Moses' warning. Israel is spared the storm, while every unprotected person, animal, and crop outside the land of Goshen suffers devastation. Pharaoh for the first time confesses his wrongheadedness, and his guilt, and his people's guilt, and promises Moses and Israel with determination, "I *will* send you out; you shall certainly stay no longer." But once more, after the storm, Pharaoh "steeled his mind," along with the unconvinced members of his court. And this time, apparently, it was without any interference from Yahweh. Thus once more, Israel remained stuck in Egypt.

In the eighth and ninth of the mighty acts, Yahweh again prevents what appears to be impending belief and surrender by Pharaoh. The eighth mighty act brings upon Egypt a vast blanket of swarming locusts that proceeds to devour the sprouting vegetation which has escaped the devastating hailstorm (10:1-20). The prediction of this agricultural last straw brings an additional breakthrough in the belief of all Pharaoh's closest advisers, his courtiers, who ask, "Just how long is this impasse to bring ruin upon us?" They advocate compliance with Yahweh's demand for Israel's release. Pharaoh appears once again to be weakening, but the negotiations break down because of his insistence that only the "able-bodied men" go out of Egypt to worship, a condition designed to prevent Israel's departure for good.

Therefore the locust swarm arrives, and Pharaoh calls for Moses and Aaron, confesses his guilt, and asks for prayer to Yahweh for forgiveness. When this prayer is made, however, and the locusts are gone, Yahweh once more intervenes, preventing Pharaoh's belief and thus his further cooperation. The ninth mighty act, the descent of an eerie darkness over the entire land of Egypt (except for the places of Israel's dwelling), follows much the same pattern, albeit more briefly (10:21-29). Pharaoh, groping in the thick darkness along with his people, sends for Moses and makes the greatest concession to that point: All Israel may go out to worship Yahweh, leaving behind only their livestock. When Moses refuses even this condition, before Pharaoh can make any response of his own, Yahweh again makes his mind obstinate, and he orders Moses to get out and never to return, on pain of death.

The tenth mighty act is announced by Yahweh as "one final stroke of judgment" that will prompt Pharaoh to allow, indeed to *demand,* an unrestricted exodus (11:1-10). Pharaoh's response to Moses' report of this announcement is not given, though Moses' furious departure from Pharaoh (11:8e) and the summary reference to Yahweh intervening to make Pharaoh's heart obstinate (11:9-10) leave no doubt as to what it was. When the tenth mighty act befalls Egypt, and the firstborn of man and beast alike have been struck dead, the final breakthrough is made. Pharaoh grants Israel unconditional permission to leave Egypt. He even requests, in what may be taken as his own confession of belief, "bless even me" (12:32d). There is now no interference from Yahweh, and at last the Exodus takes place, to the great relief of all the surviving Egyptians.

As we have seen already, however, Yahweh intervenes yet once more, even *after* the Exodus has taken place, to the utter panic of Israel and then the total destruction of Pharaoh and his elite chariot corps. This ultimate proof of Yahweh's Presence to Pharaoh can hardly be for Pharaoh's benefit, since it includes Pharaoh's death. Further, while Yahweh's accelerating pressure on Pharaoh makes sense so long as Pharaoh arrogantly doubts Yahweh's power, if not his existence, why would Yahweh himself prevent Pharaoh from making the moves of faith Yahweh has been attempting to bring Pharaoh to make? The contemporary reader may well wonder why mention of such incredible and miraculous reverses have been given no notice in the amply kept Egyptian records of the eighteenth and the nineteenth dynasties. And more important still, how could Yahweh use another human being, even one as apparently narcissistic and unpleasant as Pharaoh, as a pawn to prove a point to *Israel,* a people both separate from and a burden to Egypt?

The answer to these varied questions is one. To understand it, we must open ourselves to the very different context from which and for which this sequence of story was originally written. To begin with, what we have here must be interpreted as a theological confession of belief, and not as an historical record in narrative form. Whatever historical core may lie behind any of the sequence of story in the book of Exodus, that story in its present form is mythopoeic narrative, a sequence of confession in symbols, the presentation of the truth that is more true than simple fact. That there was an Egypt, a sojourn there of some of Abraham's descendants, an oppression of those descendants by a new and unfavorable dynasty, an ensuing conflict and an eventual separation, even an escape, can hardly be doubted. But that historical core, long since lost to us irretrievably in centuries of layers of confessional overlay, is not the concern of the sequence of story of Exodus. We read these lines too much as we would a newspaper account, asking of them the questions such an account might stimulate. We need rather to read them as we would read a hymn, a prayer, a credo, a sermon written by Dante or Shakespeare or Milton.

What happens to the Pharaoh in Yahweh's proving of his Presence is similar to what happens to Job in Yahweh's proving of the integrity of "my servant Job." We are told at the beginning of the book of Job that Job is nonpareil in all the earth, "an innocent and righteous man who has reverence for God and turns his back to evil" (Job 1:8; 2:3). All that is to come upon him is a demonstration of that integrity—so we are told throughout the sequence of story proving Yahweh's Presence that Yahweh's purpose is, precisely, that proof. It is a proof in four dimensions, as I have indicated already. Yet it is, in a way, a proof beyond those dimensions, a universalized proof, in which the Pharaoh of

Egypt is a symbol of the great sea monster of the deep, defeated by Yahweh in the ordering which made life on earth a possibility, and in which Israel is a symbol of every and any people of faith, of whatever time and of whatever place.

This sequence of story announces that God is, that God *is* here, and that his Presence means help, and rescue, and the eventual triumph, on his terms and by his schedule, of his intention. To ask whether God actually uses (and abuses) one human being, no matter how nasty that person might be, to teach a lesson to another human being, or to many other human beings, is to think of God in blatantly anthropomorphic terms, and thus to misunderstand him completely.

We are here dealing with theology, exuberantly confessed. To say that those who composed and compiled the sequence of story of the book of Exodus have presented us with a picture of God that troubles us is far more a condemnation of the narrowness of *our* view and far more an indictment of the poverty of our theological imagination than it is of theirs. The question, "What really happened at the sea of reeds?" is not only irrelevant to the sequence of story and the sequence of memory in Exodus, it is a question that diverts us altogether from the purpose and impact of those sequences. It is a question that reveals an adult weakness to use intellect, and then, inevitably, emotion, in the contemplation of texts for which only faith is an adequate resource. The real happening at the sea was the proof of Yahweh's Presence, the demonstration that Yahweh is here, revealing his Presence in his deeds. The Hebrew singers and storytellers used the language of their time to tell us about it. Our attempts to read that language only as we read the language of our time is at best ignorant and lazy, and at worst an avoidance for selfish reasons of what the biblical story is actually saying to us about God's Presence and God's salvation.

God providing and guiding by his Presence

As Israel journeys onward from the rescue at the sea into the wilderness, and heads toward the place where they are to meet Yahweh in worship, his proof to them of his Presence is augmented. The provision involves physical nourishment (meeting the need of both food and water) and protection from marauding enemies. The guidance involves direction through a barren, uncharted desert and mountain land to the place where Yahweh would present himself to them. This further demonstration of Yahweh's Presence is a testimony of the continuation of his providence in the election of his covenant people.

Interwoven with these themes of demonstration, provision and guidance, is the theme of Israel's dissatisfaction, set forth in the sequence of story by the narratives of bickering, complaint, and rebellion, narratives that extend beyond the book of Exodus into the book of Numbers (Num 11, 13-14, 16-17, 20). This interweaving is in effect a continuation of the tension in the sequence of story created first by the reluctance of Moses, then continued by the stubbornness of the Egyptians, especially that of Pharaoh—both on his own and also as a result of Yahweh's interference. Whatever Yahweh attempts, in the pursuit of his purpose with and for Israel, there is always opposition of some kind from some quarter. From the beginning, however, we know by faith how this story will come out, and that no opposition to Yahweh's intention and providence can come to any ultimate triumph. Indeed, the narrative device of this section of the sequence of story of Exodus is that Israel's need and Israel's opposition serve only to call forth further demonstrations of Yahweh's already proven Presence.

The first such complaint calling forth a demonstration arises from a need for potable water (15:22-27). Arriving at a source of water after three days' dry travel, Israel "grumbled against Moses" when they found that water too bitter to drink. Moses called out to Yahweh for help in this crisis, and Yahweh showed him a kind of wood that would remove the water's bitterness. The wood, like Moses' staff, is a symbol of Yahweh's miracle-making power. When the water became potable, Yahweh, his Presence in provision thus demonstrated, invited Israel to make a response. It is a revelation and a response that seems almost to be a preview of Sinai:

> At that very spot, he [Yahweh] established for them a requirement and a divine guidance and there he put them on trial; thus he said, "If you will pay careful attention to the voice of Yahweh your God, and do the right thing according to *his* standard, and be obedient to his commandments, and meet all his requirements, all the diseases that I put upon the Egyptians I will not put upon you: for I am Yahweh your healer."
>
> (Exod 15:25–26)

On the one hand, this assertion and promise of Yahweh is a reminder of the Presence-proving mighty acts in Egypt; on the other hand, it is an anticipation of the Sinai revelation *and* the Sinai covenant. The provision of drinkable water demonstrates Yahweh's Presence with Israel in the wilderness, and more, it attests to the continuing effectiveness of his providential care. That Presence and the guidance and provision it effects raise the question of an appropriate response. And Yahweh's statement sets forth the options of response, specifying the standard accompaniments of ancient Near Eastern covenant-making: blessing (in this case, protection and healing) for obedience and judgment for disobedience. The statement even ends with the statement with which the Sinai revelation of covenant requirement begins, "I am Yahweh" (15:26 *vis-à-vis* 20:2).

The second complaint of Israel in the wilderness is a cry for food. What had become of the flocks and herds Moses had so insisted on bringing out of Egypt (10:24–26, "not a hoof is to remain here") after only six weeks (16:1) of journey we are not told. But the grumbling against Moses and Aaron was unanimous: "you have brought us out into this wilderness to kill this whole crowd by starvation!" The people initially address this complaint to Moses and Aaron as a direction of access, not of accusation. That is, the real object of complaint (and the only one who can provide any remedy for it) is Yahweh. As Moses says: "Not against us are your grumblings, but against Yahweh" (16:8).

Thus again does Yahweh demonstrate the Presence he has proven by providing for Israel's need—Israel's complaints are presented throughout the sequence of story not as stimuli to Yahweh's provision, but as embarrassing lapses of mistrust and even unbelief. Israel was told, "Approach the Presence of Yahweh." When they turned to face the wilderness (the direction of their travel), Yahweh's glory—his *kabod* or Presence—appeared in a cloud (16:10), and Moses was told to say to Israel,

"Between dusk and dawn, you are to eat meat, and in the morning you are to be stuffed with bread; then you will know by experience that I am Yahweh your God."

(Exod 16:12)

The remedy of Israel's need is anticipated in this promise, in terms reflecting the almost humorous excess of Israel's complaint, and the purpose of that remedy is stated succinctly: The Presence is to be demonstrated by provision, and Israel is to know that Yahweh *is*, and is *here*, by their experience of his providence.

That very evening the promise of meat was fulfilled, and in the morning that followed, so also was the promise of bread—a double demonstration of Yahweh's providential Presence. Both the quails and manna are clearly regarded, wherever mentioned in the Bible (see also Num 11; Ps 78:23-29; Ps 105:40; John 6:31-33; 1 Cor 10:2-4), as miraculously provided. Attempts to explain them as naturalistic phenomena of some sort are inappropriate, as misplaced as are the similar attempts to explain the mighty acts in Egypt.

The quails are only briefly mentioned in the sequence of story of the book of Exodus; a fuller account of their arrival, their gathering, and their consumption is given in the parallel, but expanded, narrative of Numbers 11. The manna is described much more fully here, and much more briefly in Numbers 11. The manna was entirely strange to the Israelites—thus their name for it, *man hu*, "what is it?" They regarded it as a kind of miracle bread, a view enhanced by its miraculous adequacy to their daily need and by its miraculous multiplication for the sabbath, when they were not to harvest it. And Yahweh gave instructions that one day's ration of it for one person be kept so that the generations of Israel yet to come could see for themselves this demonstration of Yahweh's providing Presence.

As the journey toward Yahweh's mountain continued, a second water crisis arose, at a place called Rephidim, designated by Exodus 19:1-2 and Numbers 33:15 as the final place of encampment before Sinai. This time, there is no water of any kind, and again the people grumble against Moses. They accuse him once more of an Exodus that can only end in death, this time of thirst (17:3; in 14:11-12, they expected death at the hands of the pursuing Egyptians; in 16:3, death by starvation).

Yet again, however, Yahweh's proven Presence is demonstrated, this time as Yahweh directs Moses to "a rock in Horeb" on which he will be standing, and which yields a spring of fresh water when Moses, following Yahweh's instruction, strikes it with his rod. The designation of this rock as "in Horeb" connects this miracle of supply with the mountain of Yahweh's revelation of his Presence to Moses, and it also confirms the proximity of the wilderness destination toward which Moses is leading Israel. Because of their complaining, even in the face of all they have experienced, Moses calls the place of their encampment "Testing and Dissatisfaction" (*Massah* and *Meribah*).

The justification of this accusation by descriptive name is a trenchant summary of Israel's unbelievable disbelief and an indication of the continuing tension of the sequence of story of the book of Exodus: They had asked, "Is Yahweh present with us, or not?" He had promised to be present, of course. And he had proven that Presence, beyond any reasonable doubt and beyond even the Pharaoh's divinely pressured doubt. He had demonstrated that Presence, by his provision of water and meat and bread in the barrenness of the wilderness. And yet his own chosen people, the elect descendants of Abraham, those who had seen it all with their own eyes, could still somehow doubt, and actually ask, "Is Yahweh present with us, or not?" Already their greatest doubt and their most incredible disobedience are in view, and beyond that the litany of doubts and disobedience of every disbelieving believer throughout the range of the Old Testament story, the biblical story, and even our own story of belief and disbelief.

Also at Rephidim, Israel encountered the first in what was to be a series of armed enemies intent on blocking their way. Once again, Yahweh must demonstrate his proven Presence, this time by enabling Israel's forces to defeat the forces of Amalek, who had joined battle with them. Moses took up a position on a hilltop overlooking the battlefield and lifted his hands, perhaps holding "the staff of God." Israel was able to prevail against Amalek only as long as Moses continued holding up his hands; thus when Moses grew tired, Aaron and Hur, the son of Caleb, supported his hands until Joshua had defeated the Amalekites. The involvement of Yahweh in this deliverance is emphasized not only by the reference to the staff of God, and by the divine encouragement (or perhaps even power) transmitted through Moses' uplifted hands. More specifically it is underlined still by Yahweh's promissory curse utterly to "efface the recollection of Amalek," a curse Moses is to write down in "the book" (perhaps "The Book of the Wars of Yahweh" quoted in Numbers 21:14–15).

Yahweh's involvement is also emphasized by the altar named "Yahweh is my standard," a name explained so: "Because a hand has been against Yah's throne, there will be battle between Yahweh and Amalek, from one generation to another" (17:15–16). The interference of Amalek with Israel's progress toward Horeb/Sinai is taken by Yahweh as an attack upon himself, and it becomes an opportunity for yet another demonstration of his Presence with Israel, this time in providential protection and the enhancement of military skills and strength.

The final narratives of Yahweh's provision and guidance in the sequence of story in the book of Exodus both involve Moses' father-in-law, Jethro/Reuel/Hobab. The first of those narratives (18:1–12) is a narrative of reunion; the second of them (18:13–27) is a narrative of guidance. The first one provides a logical conclusion to the story of Moses' departure from his family in Midian and his return to Egypt to bring forth his people Israel. The second is an important anticipation of what is to transpire in Yahweh's presentation of his Presence to Israel assembled at Sinai. And it is also an instructive memory of the beginnings of Israel's legal system—one that is illuminating for the sequence of requirement extending from Exodus 20 through Exodus 23 (see pp. 86–93).

The narrative of reunion is an appropriate ending of the Exodus story, with its summary, for Jethro's benefit, of all that had transpired in Egypt and at the sea. In thematic terms also, it is the important conclusion to the separation motif set forth repeatedly in the sequence of story in the book of Genesis and hinted at in the account of Moses' discovery of home in Midian (Exod 2:16-22). This narrative, therefore, seems logically in place.

The narrative of guidance, however, seems, at least in terms of a logical sequence, to be out of place, presupposing as it does the application to living of the requirements and instructions of Yahweh (see pp. 89-93) that have yet to be given in the Exodus sequence of story. Indeed, it would appear to fit the sequence of story better following Exodus 24, after the covenant with Yahweh has been solemnized, or even following Exodus 34, after that covenant has been renewed and Israel is making ready to depart Sinai. This problem of sequence cannot have been overlooked by the compilers of the book of Exodus, so the narrative of guidance must have been placed where it is for some good reason. I suggest that the reason is thematic and theological.

The separation motif is reflected in the stories of Cain (Gen 4:10-16), Hagar and Ishmael (Gen 21:8-21), Keturah's sons (Gen 25:1-6), and Esau (Gen 25:19-34; 27:1-45; 28:6-9; 32:3-6; 33:1-20). Over against these stories of nomadic wandering in the East are the stories of those who settle into a life in locations more or less fixed in the land promised: Seth (Gen 5:3), Isaac (Gen 24:1-10; 25:6), and Jacob (Gen 28:1-5; 33:12-18; 35:5-15). The only meeting in later life of the half-brothers Ishmael and Isaac was at their father's burial at the cave of Machpelah (Gen 25:9, 11-18). Jacob and Esau, following their reunion upon Jacob's return from Paddan-aram, were not able to dwell in the same area (Gen 36:6-8). The subsequent journey of Jacob and his sons to Egypt, following the travel and the prosperity there of Joseph, amounts to a further separation from the Esau branch of the family, nowhere mentioned in the Old Testament as having any connection whatever with the famine in Canaan, the sojourn in Egypt, or the Exodus from there. At the beginning of the sequence of story in Exodus, therefore, the family of Abraham, Yahweh's election-people, stands divided, separated into two branches by the greed, jealousy, and strife that followed them. Consequently, it is a matter of urgency that the family be reunited before Yahweh's great presentation to them of his Presence, his invitation of them into covenantal response, and his fulfillment for them of his promise of land.

So Moses becomes the medium of reconciliation and reunion of the two parts of Abraham's family: His newfound family in Midian turns out to be, in what I have elsewhere called "one of those remarkable connections so recurrent in the Bible,"[20] just the other branch of his ancestral family. Jethro becomes the symbol of the Cain/Keturah/Ishmael/Esau side of the family—the nomadic, "Eastern," trans-Jordan side. Aaron becomes the symbol of the Seth/Sarah/Isaac/Jacob side, the settled, "Western," promised-land side. In the communion meal symbolizing this reunion, for this reason, the principal figures are Jethro and Aaron. Moses is not mentioned as even having a part in that meal, and it is Jethro, not Aaron, who receives and distributes the meat and the bread (Exod 18:12).

The references to Moses' two sons at the beginning of this account of reunion are a further testimony to these connections. Jethro has kept Moses' family during his absence; he now brings Zipporah and the two boys (only one is mentioned in Exodus 2:21-22 and 4:25, though 4:20 refers to "sons") to rejoin Moses "in the wilderness where he was camped, there at the mountain of God" (18:5). The interpretation of Gershom's name, "a stranger have I been in a land foreign to me" is repeated (see 2:22) in reference to Moses' stay in Egypt, and the second son's name is given as Eliezer, "my God is help," in reference to the deliverance of the Exodus: "The God of my father was my help; thus he rescued me from Pharaoh's sword" (18:4).

Jethro is reported to have heard about the Exodus, and perhaps also the mighty acts of Yahweh and the demonstrations of his proven Presence—for that reason he came to Sinai, bringing Moses' family to him. Even so, however, Jethro quite naturally has to hear the wonderful report at first hand, from Moses himself. Upon hearing it, Jethro blesses Yahweh, summarizing Moses' proof and demonstration of the Presence of Yahweh, and making a confession of faith in Yahweh that is all his own: "Now I know for certain that Yahweh is greater than all the gods" (18:11a). This confession, and the fact that Jethro presides at the communion meal—when added to his role in guiding Moses in applying the principles of life in covenant with Yahweh, and considered with the fact that Yahweh presents himself to Moses and Israel in the territory of Midianite nomadism—has given rise to the supposition that Moses first learned about Yahweh from Jethro.

The narrative of guidance in Exodus 18:13–17, however logically a *non sequitur* it may be, meshes with the preparation of Israel for Yahweh's presentation of his Presence. Just as the two sides of the family of Abraham need to be reunited before Yahweh comes to them, so also does Moses need instruction in the application to life of Yahweh's requirements and instruction. Once again, it is Jethro who stands out as the figure of authority, Jethro who gives Moses pointed and detailed counsel, counsel Moses is reported as following to the letter and without question. Indeed, Jethro represents the counsel he gives as a divine command (18:23), the obedience of which will ensure God's Presence (18:19). The whole impression of this narrative is consonant with the picture of Jethro as Moses' mentor, and Aaron's, in all matters relating both to the worship of Yahweh and also to life in obedience with Yahweh's expectation.

The stimulus for Jethro's advice to Moses is the obviously impossible workload the people's needs have placed upon Moses. They must wait long hours for Moses to get to them and their requests, and the number of them needing an interpretation of the divine "requirements and instructions" is rapidly exceeding the time and energy Moses has to give. Moses' explanation is that the inquiries of the people are actually inquiries of God. The implication is that only Moses, as the intermediary passing along Yahweh's instructions, is in a position, or has the authority, to deal with them.

Jethro's advice is linked to this valid point. Moses must continue his role as authoritative intermediary, but he must save his time and strength for that unique task by delegating responsibility to carefully chosen "men of ability" and integrity for the routine, repeated problems for which divine guidance has already been obtained and successfully applied. Jethro says,

"Every complex problem, they shall bring to you, and every routine problem *they* shall deal with. Thus will things be lighter for you: they will carry the load with you. If you follow this procedure, as God charges you to do, then you will be able to stand up under the pressure, and all this people as well will go to their own place satisfied." (18:22b–23)

This advice Moses followed to the letter, and when he had selected these "leaders" and "set them in charge" of units of the people of decreasing size from a thousand to ten,

They decided cases for the people on a continuing basis: the difficult problems, they brought straight to Moses; every routine problem, *they* dealt with. (18:26)

The Sequence of Story 55

What we are given here, albeit in a somewhat developed form, is an ancient tradition of the origin and working of the legal system of Israel, with its Ancient Near Eastern distinction between laws of principle, universal in application (apodictic laws), and laws of situation, restricted in application (casuistic laws) and based on precedents and solutions previously successful.

The theme that has drawn these Jethro narratives to their present location, as I have said already, is the preparation of Israel for Yahweh's presentation to them of his Presence. That preparation comes first in the reunion of the divided descendants of Abraham, second in the instruction Jethro gives for worshiping Yahweh and for applying to life the principles of living in covenant with him—principles soon to be revealed in the sequence of story as an integral part of Yahweh's presentation of his Presence. By placing these Jethro narratives here, *before* the giving of the requirements and instructions with which they are in one way or another concerned, the storytellers of Exodus have given a striking emphasis to the need for special preparation for the unique moments of faith. And they have, at the same time, given an important reminder of the desert origins of Israel's faith.

God presenting his Presence

Yahweh's presentation of his Presence to Israel while the nation was gathered on the plain before Horeb/Sinai is the very center of the sequence of story of the book of Exodus. In a way, it is the center also of the sequence of story of the Old Testament, and of the Bible, taken as a whole, for the coming of God is *the* subject of the biblical story.

The account of the presentation, the event toward which the entire sequence of story of Exodus has been moving, is resonant with an excitement the contemporary reader tends too often to miss. After so many weeks of turmoil in Egypt;

after the heart-stopping suspense of the final, unbelievable release, the hope-shattering pursuit and the miraculous rescue at the sea; after the frightening shortages and wonderful provisions of the wilderness; and after the arrival of Israel at Horeb/Sinai (the mountain about which Moses had told them so often and toward which he had led them so urgently), the people's expectancy had to have been at manic levels.

The narrative of Yahweh's self-revelation—even at this distance, and despite much rearrangement and some overlay—still tingles with excitement. It continues a suspense that has been building from the beginning of the sequence of story, and sets in motion an imagery that echoes in every Old Testament reference to the coming of God. Following the further notice (cf. 18:5) of Israel's arrival at Sinai, we are told that "Moses went up towards God." As it now stands, Exodus 19 includes at this point both a covenant-renewal sequence of memory (19:3b-6), a response to it (19:7-8), and a further authorization of Moses (19:9). The narrative of Yahweh's presentation of his Presence thus actually begins with his instructions for the preparation of Israel (19:10-15).

These instructions, which serve to heighten the drama of the moment of self-revelation, make the point that the protocols of dress and readiness for the arrival of Yahweh's Presence are a reflection of the specialness of the experience. The people are to be "set apart for holiness" by:

1. washing their clothes,
2. contemplating the experience before them for two days,
3. learning the boundaries of Yahweh's powerful holiness, boundaries they are not to cross, upon pain of death, and
4. abstaining from sexual intercourse—in keeping with the requirements reflected elsewhere in such passages as 1 Samuel 21:1-6 and Leviticus 15:16-33.

The Sequence of Story   57

Since both ritual uncleanness and holiness are regarded in the Old Testament as communicable by any physical contact, even an indirect one, the boundaries of the people's approach to Yahweh's mountain were to be protected by the stoning or shooting (by archers or slingers) of any person or beast who violated them.

These preparations made, and these prohibitions observed, on the third day after Israel's arrival at Sinai, at daybreak, the awesome event, long anticipated, happened. The report of it even now rumbles with an ominous, distant thunder and echoes with the eerie vibrato of the ram's horn drawing nearer. We can almost feel the prickly static of the lightning near at hand, and find ourselves half eager and half reluctant to peer through the brightness of its licking illumination into the thick cloud and heavy smoke as the whole mountain shakes beneath our feet. The experience of Horeb/Sinai is *our* experience. The sequence of story in Exodus puts us there, if we read it with faith.

Despite Moses' intermediary role the important original insistence of this account—that Yahweh's presentation of his Presence was to *all* Israel—still shines through. This essential emphasis is clearly made by (1) the preparation of all the people for the advent of the third day, a preparation justified by the statement, "They are to be completely ready by the third day, because on the third day Yahweh will come down, before the eyes of the whole people, onto Mount Sinai" (19:11); (2) the report that, when the third day arrived, "Moses led the people out from the camp to encounter God" (19:17a); (3) the reaction of the people to their experience of Yahweh's self-revelation of his Presence, "and all the people were experiencing the rumblings of thunder and the bolts of lightning and the sound of the ram's horn and the mountain smoking: and as the people took it in, they trembled and drew some distance back" (20:18); and (4) the continuing tradition that Yahweh's own voice, sounding forth from the fire, was heard by all the people: "These words [the Ten Commandments] Yahweh spoke to all your congregation before the mountain, from within the fire, the cloud and the heavy darkness, a great voice." (Deut 5:22; see also Deut 4:11-14, 32-33, 35-36; 5:4, 23-26).

It is an experience absolutely unique in the biblical record. The only narrative even generally parallel to it is the story in Acts 2 of the advent, upon the confused disciples, of the Holy Spirit of God. Well might Israel have been terrified to the point of death, even *before* they heard Yahweh speaking. And then that voice came—who can imagine the sound of it? What it spoke was this:

"I am Yahweh, your God,
　　who brought you forth from the land of Egypt. . . .
You are not to have other gods.
You are not to make for yourself a shaped image. . . .
You are not to employ the name of Yahweh your God
　　to an empty purpose. . . .
Remember the sabbath day. . . .
Give honor to your father and your mother. . . .
You are not to kill.
You are not to commit adultery.
You are not to steal.
You are not to give against your neighbor
　　a lying testimony.
You are not to desire for yourself
　　the house of your neighbor."
　　　　　　　　　　　　(Exod 20:2-4a, 7a, 8a, 12a, 13-17a)

This succinct form of the Ten Commandments is my attempt to suggest their original and briefer statement, a compactness that justifies the designation "the Ten Words" in Exodus 34:28 and Deuteronomy 4:13 and 10:4. We may reasonably surmise an even briefer, more memorable form for these ten principles of living in covenant relationship with Yahweh, especially in view of their inclusion in the sequence of story of Yahweh's self-revelation of his Presence on Mount Horeb/Sinai. As that story now stands, both in the book of Exodus and in other recollections of it in Deuteronomy 4 and 5 and elsewhere in the Old Testament, these ten principles *are* that presentation—an integral part, indeed *the* essential part—of Yahweh's theophany to Israel. They are *not* to be taken out of the sequence of story as disruptive of it (as some literary critics have done) for they *are* that story, not an intrusion into it.

Their beginning is a repetition of Yahweh's self-presentation ("I am Yahweh"), a link with the fathers ("your God"), and a summary of the proof and demonstration of his Presence ("who brought you forth from the land of Egypt"). Their order describes the tension of revelation and response that the Horeb/Sinai presentation of Presence is: The first four commandments are principles guiding Israel's relationship to Yahweh; the last six are principles guiding Israel's relationships to one another and to the larger human family because of their relationship with Yahweh. These commandments are the fundamental pattern for Israel's response to Yahweh's self-revelation, through their daily worship and by their daily behavior.

The statement "I am Yahweh" is a declaration, as we have seen, of Yahweh's real and active Presence in Israel's midst. The Ten Words that follow are an explanation by expectation of what and how Yahweh *is*, and is *here*. They identify and describe the Yahweh who has come to Israel by stating what he requires of those who know that he is and *is* here. They set forth a covenant of being with the God who is—Israel is to be a certain way because of the way Yahweh is—"the One Who Always Is." They are a gift to an Israel needing to know how to live in God's company.

Yahweh's theophanic address to Israel is therefore

introduced with a statement of his nature ("I am Yahweh") and continues with a statement of their identity ("your God, who brought you forth from the land of Egypt"). It then moves on to a compact summary of what this means for their living. The first of Yahweh's expectations is absolute priority and total loyalty. Those who are to be as his people are to have no other gods—they are to seek out and worship him alone.

The next three expectations are descriptions of how Israel is and is not to express devotion to Yahweh. They are not to use any shaped image as a means of focus for their worship, individual or corporate. They must worship him as he is, mysterious and invisible, and not as they might envision him to be or want him to be. They are to be completely serious about Yahweh's Presence among them, respecting his Presence as symbolized by the gift of his name, Yahweh. That name and Presence is not to be used "to empty purpose." In relation to this priority—this acceptance of Yahweh as he presents himself, and this respect for the Presence declared by his name—Israel is also to observe without lapse the final day of each week (the day of stopping kept by Yahweh himself) as a day that belongs to Yahweh. It is a day set aside for remembering who he is so that Israel may know and remember who *they* are.

As the second, third, and fourth of the commandments are extensions of the first commandment, so the final six commandments are built on the foundation laid by the first four. As Yahweh is to be honored for his priority above all life, so one's father and mother are to be honored for their priority, in Yahweh's ordering, in the lives of their children. Though this fifth commandment has frequently been directed (by parents especially) toward children, its primary address here is toward adult children, those who are responsible above all for obedience to the covenant, those who are to guide the young and keep the old.

The sixth of Yahweh's words is a prohibition against any

act of killing, the introduction of violence into the covenant community. The prohibition is not against the killing of war or capital punishment, both of which the law of the Old Testament permits. It refers to a standard of conduct within the covenant community that Yahweh expects, and is thus primarily a religious prohibition and not a social one. The same can be said of the seventh of Yahweh's words. The prohibition against adultery here is religious rather than social: Adultery is a denial of Israel's specialness and, therefore, a denial of Yahweh's specialness. For this reason, adultery becomes the charge against the covenant community for the worship of idols (Exod 32:21-34; Isa 57:1-13; Jer 3:6-9; Ezek 23:36-49); adultery was for Israel a turning away from commitment to Yahweh. So also the eighth of Yahweh's words is a prohibition against an activity that breaches Israel's unique human-divine relationship by breaching human relationships through the destruction of trust. This commandment forbids stealing of any kind.

The last two of Yahweh's Ten Words prohibit, respectively, the compromise of the reputation of another member of the covenant community, through a lying testimony, and the compromise of one's own integrity, through an obsessive lusting after something that belongs to another.

The reputation of one's neighbor in the covenant community was important to that neighbor for obvious reasons. It was important to the potential slanderer because of the importance to himself as well as to the whole community of congenial relationships. Above all, Yahweh's reputation as God of the community was also at stake. Behavior inimical to Yahweh's expectation would erode the witness Israel was called to be.

The tenth of the Ten Words similarly prohibits behavior that may lead to the disintegration of personal integrity, and so is, in a way, a kind of summary commandment. Desiring for oneself that which belongs to another could provide the gateway to the violation of any other one, or even to all, of the other commandments. As in the commandment preceding it, this commandment, too, is first of all religious and not social in its concern.

The expanded statement of the second, third, fourth, fifth, and tenth of the commandments is an indication of which of the fundamental principles of living in covenant with Yahweh gave Israel the greatest difficulty. The longer the statement, the more detailed its specification of people, reasons, or rewards for obedience, the more probable is a history of avoidance, loophole chasing and rationalization. In the second, fourth, and tenth commandments in particular, the seams of expansion are especially obvious, and they indicate a history of struggle on Israel's part to become the people Yahweh desired them to be.

These expansions belong, however, to the sequence of requirement in the book of Exodus and not to the theophanic address of Yahweh to Israel presented as so central a part of the sequence of story. That sequence is best read as a dramatic continuum moving from Moses' preparation of Israel for Yahweh's theophany (the central feature of which is his statement of the Ten Words) to the report of Israel's reaction after experiencing this event and then to their response to the event in the making, breaking and remaking of covenantal commitment.

The sequence of Yahweh's presentation of his Presence to Israel at Horeb/Sinai thus moves from 19:1–3a to 19:10–20a to 20:1–21. The powerful tension of this sequence is far more obvious when presented in a serial reading, omitting the interpolations made for a variety of reasons:

In the third month of the Exodus of the sons of Israel from the land of Egypt, on the very day they came to the wilderness of Sinai . . . Moses went up towards God. . . . So Yahweh said to Moses, "Go to the people, and set them apart for holiness today and to-morrow. They are to wash their clothes. They are to be completely ready by the third day, because on the third day Yahweh will come down, before the eyes of the whole people, onto Mount Sinai. You are to establish boundaries for the people all around, warning, 'Be careful about going up onto the mountain, or even touching its outcropping: all who touch the mountain will certainly be executed—no hand is to touch him; rather is he to be stoned to death or mortally shot, whether beast or man he is not to live.' With the drawn-out signal of the bell-horn, they are to come up to the mountain."

So Moses went down from the mountain to the people. Then he set the people apart for holiness, and they washed their clothes. Next, he said to the people, "Be completely ready by the third day. Do not have intercourse with a woman."

And so it was, on the third day, when the morning was breaking, that there were rumblings of thunder and flashes of lightning, and a heavy cloud upon the mountain. The sound of a ram's horn was very strong, so much so that all the people in the camp were terrified. Then Moses led the people out from the camp to encounter God. They took a position at the bottom of the mountain. The whole of Mount Sinai was smoking from the Presence of Yahweh, who came down upon it in the fire—indeed, the smoke of it boiled up like smoke from the pottery-kiln, and the whole mountain shook violently. The sound of the ram's horn meanwhile was moving, and growing very strong. . . .

Thus Yahweh came down upon Mount Sinai, to the top of the mountain. . . . Then Yahweh[21] spoke all these words, saying,

"I am Yahweh, your God, who brought you forth
from the land of Egypt. . . .
You are not to have other gods. . . .
You are not to make for yourself a shaped
   image. . . .
You are not to employ the name of Yahweh
   your God to empty purpose. . . .
Remember the sabbath day. . . .
Give honor to your father and your
   mother. . . .
You are not to kill.
You are not to commit adultery.
You are not to steal.
You are not to give against your neighbor
   a lying testimony.
You are not to desire for yourself
   the house of your neighbor. . . ."

And all the people were experiencing the rumblings of
thunder and the bolts of lightning and the sound of the
ram's horn and the mountain smoking: and as the people took it in, they trembled and drew some distance
back. Then they said to Moses, "You speak with us, and
we promise we'll hear—but don't let God keep speaking with us, lest we die!" But Moses replied to the people, "Don't be afraid, for it is with the purpose of giving
you the experience that God has come, so that reverence for him might grip you and prevent you from sinning." So the people took a position at a distance, while
Moses approached the thick cloud where God was.

The conclusion to the story of Yahweh's self-revelation
on Horeb/Sinai is thus a brief notice of Israel's response to
this fascinating and frightening event, an anticipation of the

role Moses is to have (as Yahweh's spokesman to them and as their spokesman to Yahweh) and also a hint of what is to come in the way of their response, both positive and negative. That two-part response forms the conclusion to the sequence of story in the book of Exodus, and to that double conclusion we now turn.

Israel responding to God's Presence

Israel's response to Yahweh's presentation of his Presence to them at Horeb/Sinai follows immediately, in the sequence of story, after the narrative of frightened response in Exod 20:18-21. The large block of material explicating and applying the Ten Words, Exodus 20:22-23:33, is a part of the sequence of requirement of the book of Exodus, inserted at a point appropriate to its purpose but nevertheless posing an inevitable disruption of the dramatic flow and tension of the sequence of story. So also Exodus 25:1-31:18, a part of the sequence of memory of the book of Exodus, is intrusive of the continuation of the narrative of Israel's response—it too is inserted into the story at a logically appropriate point, but these chapters of instruction and specification of the media of the worship of Yahweh obscure, in their present location, and with their emphasis on worship and daily life in commitment to Yahweh, the momentum of the story of Israel's response.

That momentum is set off by Yahweh's appearance to, and address of, Israel. It then progresses from a loyal response to a negation of that response (in a betrayal that is disloyalty), to a crisis in which Yahweh threatens to withdraw altogether his Presence just given, and finally to a resolution of that crisis and a renewal of covenant relationship. The insertion of the collection of legal-religious requirements applying the ten principles Yahweh has stated, and of the array of symbolic objects designed to aid worship in Yahweh's Presence,

66   *EXODUS*

stretches the sequence of the story of response apart at two vital points. Once the inserted material is removed, the sequence of story is immediately and obviously restored, as this reading of these verses together, in comparison with their location in the received text, makes clear:

20:21: So the people took a position at a distance, while Moses approached the thick cloud where God was.

24:1-2: Then to Moses he said, "Climb up toward Yahweh: you, and Aaron, Nadab and Abihu, and seventy of the elders of Israel, and bow down in worship at a respectful distance. Moses by himself is to come close to Yahweh—the others are not to come close, nor are the people to climb up with him."

At this point there is a narrative describing the ceremony of the entry of the people of Israel into covenant with Yahweh (24:3-8), followed by the movement up onto the mountain of the group of leaders specified in Exod 24:1, where they experience "a vision of God" and partake of a communion meal (vv 9-11). Then Yahweh calls Moses further up onto the mountain still, first with Joshua and then alone (vv 12-14). The sequence of story then continues:

24:15-18: So Moses climbed up higher on the mountain, and the cloud concealed the mountain. Thus the glory of Yahweh settled onto Mount Sinai, and the cloud concealed it six days; then on the seventh day Yahweh called out to Moses from the midst of the cloud. The spectacle of the glory of Yahweh, to the eyes of the sons of Israel, was like a consuming fire at the mountain's peak. Then Moses went into the midst of the cloud, climbing up higher on the mountain. In fact, Moses was on the mountain forty days and forty nights.

The Sequence of Story   67

32:1:   Then the people realized that Moses was long
          overdue coming down from the mountain, and so
          they came together against Aaron, and they said to
          him. "Get busy! Make gods for us who can lead us,
          because this Moses, the man who brought us up
          from the land of Egypt, we have no idea what has
          become of him."

The sequence of story in the book of Exodus continues
this narrative of rebellion and covenant breaking through its
compromising course to the account of Yahweh's mercy and
the subsequent renewal of his covenant relationship with
Israel. Here as throughout the sequence, the dominant
theme is Yahweh's Presence and the difference in living that
it demands. The thematic structure of the sequence of story
is built on the revelation, the proving, and the presentation
of that Presence. This is so to such an intense and obsessive
degree that when, suddenly and unbelievably, Israel's behavior raises the prospect of Yahweh's disappointed withdrawal,
the impact is staggering.

What Yahweh has given to Israel, above all, is himself.
Israel's doubt, because of Moses' absence, amounts to a rejection of that gift. The whole sequence of story is suddenly
reversed. Israel, alone in the wilderness, this people so newly
become God's people, can only become a nonpeople, whose
situation is far worse than it ever was in the dependent
bondage of Egypt. It is a powerful and stark presentation of
the reality of Israel's position throughout history, a paradigm
also of the church. What is the situation of a community of
faith with no faith? How can a godly people be godly if they
are God-less? What is to become of a people who are a people
only because God is among them, if God departs from them?
When absence replaces Presence what happens to hope?

The Presence of Yahweh is the keystone of the architecture of the sequence of story in Exodus, and the possibility

of its withdrawal plunges the narrative into chaos. Israel is left with no place to go and no reason to be. This shrill and panic-bringing dissonance is entirely deliberate, brilliantly achieved, and, without the additions that blunt its sharp counterpoint to most of the rest of the sequence of story in Exodus, it is powerfully effective.

The tension of the struggle in Egypt with an ambivalent Pharaoh, of the miraculous rescue at the sea, and of the various shortages and perils of the wilderness is resolved with Israel's arrival at Sinai. There, the divided family of Abraham is at long last reunited. Amidst joyous celebration, Moses prepares the people for Yahweh's arrival "on the third day." This expectation creates a new kind of tension, one only increased by Yahweh's advent and the sound of his voice from the fire and the thick cloud upon the mountain. When a terrified Israel pleads with Moses to spare them any such experience in their future, he reassures them: Yahweh's advent to them has their faith as its purpose, that they might have reverence for him, and so be prevented from sinning (Exod 20:20).

This reassurance serves the function, in the sequence of story, of anticipating, at the unlikeliest point imaginable, what is actually to occur. In other words, Yahweh's proof of his Presence, and his demonstration of it, and his Advent in presentation of it, do not work. They are somehow, incredibly, not enough for Israel.

In Egypt, when conditions grow more difficult, they complain. At the sea, when the Pharaoh's pursuit seems about to snatch failure from the arms of success, they forget all they have seen and whimper about graves. In the wilderness, when thirst and hunger overtake them, they whine as though they have never been freed, rescued, and guided—moaning about the great cuisine they enjoyed as slaves in Egypt. At Horeb/Sinai, when the event toward which Moses has drawn them (and for which they have longed and prepared themselves) actually arrives, they are terrified and plead with Moses to spare them any such encounter in the future. Indeed, they complain about their blessing as though it were a curse. How can we imagine that, with the entry of these people into covenant with Yahweh, things are to be any different? How can they hope to see more than they have seen, or experience more than they have experienced already?

The point, of course, is that they have not seen, despite their looking, and have not really experienced what has happened all around them. They are a paradigm of the community that claims to believe, yet does not, really, in every age. Their making of covenant with Yahweh, solemn and impressive though its symbolic ceremony, seems almost too good to be true following so many doubts after so many rescues and mercies. Given the sequence of story preceding it, and the terrible narrative of covenant breaking that we know will follow it, we may be excused for thinking of Joshua 24, and of Joshua's reluctance to permit Israel to enter into a covenantal commitment that he fears they will not keep.

Moses' climb up Sinai at Yahweh's command, accompanied by Aaron, his sons Nadab and Abihu, and seventy of Israel's elders has, in the present composite of the sequence of story,[22] a double purpose. First, Moses is to receive and pass along to Israel the terms, the symbols, and the ceremony of the people's entry into covenant with Yahweh. Second, Moses and Israel's leaders are to receive an enhancement of their authority as leaders in a unique, and still more intimate, experience of Yahweh's Presence.

Following Yahweh's instructions, Moses repeats to the people the guiding principles of life in covenant with Yahweh, then builds at the base of Horeb/Sinai an altar and twelve stone pillars, the former a symbol of Yahweh's Presence, the latter a symbol of the presence of each of the twelve tribes.

Next, he delegates young men to offer the wholly burned offerings and the completion sacrifices that are standard accompaniments of covenant making in the Old Testament. From these sacrifices, Moses takes the blood, dashes half of it upon the altar representing Yahweh's Presence and, after reading out "the book of the covenant," dashes the second half of the blood upon the people, with these words: "See now the blood of the covenant that Yahweh has contracted with you, a covenant made specific by all these words" (24:8). "All these words" refers both to the Ten Commandments and to the extended and specific application of them represented by the sequence of requirement of 20:22–23:33 (see pp. 89–93).

Then, well up on the mountain, Moses, Aaron, Nadab, and Abihu, and the elders (representing the "men of ability" which Jethro had counseled Moses to single out) experience by Yahweh's invitation a special vision of his Presence, and eat and drink together a meal of communion. The obvious purpose of this unique event is the equipment and authentication of Israel's leaders for the tasks of presentation, interpretation, and guidance they are to undertake. Their "seeing," their vision, of "the God of Israel" is absolutely unique in the Old Testament. What they literally see is described as "something like a mosaic pavement of lapis lazuli, like the span of the heavens in depth" (24:10). It is a composite suggestion, a reflection of the midnight blue of an endless night sky and the precious building blocks of divine dwelling places, not unlike our own "pearly gates and streets of gold."

Every word of this covenant-making narrative is, in some way, a variation of the theme of Yahweh's Presence and Israel's logical, expected, and hoped-for response. Moses is then called higher up the mountain, where he is to be given additional instructions for both Israel and the leaders, while Israel on the plain below is treated to "the spectacle of the glory of Yahweh" at the top of the mountain.

The Sequence of Story 71

The note at the very end of this narrative, that Moses was a long time up on the mountain in Yahweh's Presence, prepares us for the unexpected turn the sequence of story in the book of Exodus takes as it now moves toward its conclusion.

As we have seen already, taking the block of text inserted from the sequence of memory (Exod 25–31) out of the sequence of story restores the original, dramatic narrative. Then Exodus 24:18 and 32:1, read consecutively, present the problem. Moses' long absence gives rise once again to Israel's doubt, and then to rising panic. These are the people who doubted and feared following the ten mighty acts, the deliverance at the sea, the variety of provision and guidance in the wilderness, and even the long-expected and carefully prepared for presentation by Yahweh of his Presence at Horeb/Sinai. Now, immediately after their great experience of that moment, and despite what they have seen with their own eyes and heard with their own ears, they grow afraid with Moses gone and in that fear they ask Aaron to "make gods for us who can lead us."

Demanding golden jewelry from the people of Israel, Aaron "made a calf with a shaped sheathing." This object was received with acclamation as symbolic of the power that made possible their exodus from Egypt. Aaron's construction of an altar before this image, and his declaration of "a sacred feast day for Yahweh," make plain that Israel is here attempting to worship *Yahweh*, not some new and different deity or array of deities. Israel's sin with the golden calf is not an attempted displacement or replacement of Yahweh, but rather an attempt to worship him in ways of *their* choosing instead of in ways specified by him. They even attempt to mimic their covenant ceremony with Yahweh, offering "wholly burned offerings" and bringing "completion offerings" (cf. 24:5), but their desire for a visible symbol of their invisible God has been denied them already.

The mystery of God's holy divinity requires us to receive and to worship God on his terms, not ours. God must be met at a place, and in a manner, of *his* choosing. His choices are almost always surprising to us, precisely because *our* choices are almost always so predictably self-oriented. Our life in faith must struggle constantly to be open to his guidance, in both our worship and our commitment. The lesson of the golden calf is that self-oriented worship is always a disaster, for both faith and behavior.

In the light of the sequence of story to this point in Exodus, we can hardly be surprised at Israel's foolish abandonment of the covenantal commitment. Given the continued record of complaining, doubting, and wishy-washiness, we might well have expected this defection. Astonishment gives way to disgust in the ancient memory of the event that is preserved for us in Psalm 106:19–20:

They made a calf at Horeb,
They bowed themselves down to an overlaid image.
They swapped their Presence
    for a likeness of a grass-eating bull.

It is one more turning back, worse than all the rest, for this time Israel, and not just Yahweh, has made promises. Yahweh's Presence has brought deliverance and guidance and provision and unique relationship. Israel's selfishness has met that Presence with doubt and complaint and fear and an attempt at manipulation. The response to the revelation has turned from praise to rebellion.

The anger of Moses at this turning is predictable. The judgment of Yahweh is astonishing. Moses shatters the tablets on which Yahweh had written the Ten Words, in a graphic reflection of what Israel has done. Then he grinds the golden calf into powder, mixes it with water, and forces Israel to drink the mixture. Next, he sends the loyal Levites through the camp, swords in hand, slaying the rebels, whatever their relationship.

Finally, he returns up the mountain toward Yahweh to plead with Yahweh on Israel's behalf. Probably, Exodus 32–34 is a composite account,[23] and those various actions by Moses, along with Yahweh's responses and the interaction between the two, represent layers of tradition. In its present composite form, however, this sequence of story has a tremendous impact, with Moses' anger and almost panic-stricken attempts to correct the terrible wrong suggesting a futile anticipation of what Yahweh's judgment must inevitably be.

By every standard of ancient Near Eastern covenant making, the result of Israel's willful violation of the commitment so willingly and so solemnly made should be abandonment of the relationship, curse replacing blessing. That is exactly what Yahweh proposes to do. He is, with their violation of the terms of the covenant, under no further obligation to them. He not only *can* abandon Israel without further ado, he really *should* do so. Commitment has given way to compromise, and the response to the revelation of God's Presence has turned from praise to rebellion. There is no surprise in the severity of Yahweh's proposals of severance and destruction; the surprise is not in what Yahweh proposes to do but in what Yahweh *does* do.

At first, Yahweh proposes to bring Israel to an end as his nation, and to make of Moses alone a great nation (32:10). From this course of action Moses dissuades Yahweh by reminding him of what the Egyptians might say, "For an evil purpose he brought them out, to slaughter them in the mountains, and to obliterate them from the face of the land" (32:12), and of his promise to the Fathers of a numberless progeny and a wide land (32:13).

Next, Yahweh commands Moses and Israel to leave Horeb/Sinai, the place of his Presence, announcing that while he will send a messenger before them to clear the promised land of opposition to them, he will no longer travel in their midst or go up among them into the land he has given to their Fathers (33:1-2). This "dreadful news" is understandably received by Israel with great lamentation— here and henceforth, they put away all festive dress (33:4). They no longer have any cause for celebration, with Yahweh gone from them.

This desperate situation prompts Moses to ask Yahweh to set aside what he has proposed to do, what indeed he has every right to do, and to go up with Israel through the wilderness and into the land promised to them. Without Yahweh's Presence, this people, who have only just become a people, will be once more a nonpeople: it is only in his Presence that Moses and Israel are "separated from all the people who are upon the surface of the earth" (33:16).

And so it is that Yahweh decides what he will do with Israel (cf. 32:34 and 33:5e). Contrary to all expectation, against what Yahweh himself has said that he would do, and in violation of what is correct by all the standards of covenantal obligation, Yahweh decides to remain bound to the people who have rejected him, to go up with them in spite of their rebellion, to show them grace instead of just and fair payment, to give them blessing instead of curse.

Understandably elated, Moses boldly asks Yahweh to show him his glory, that is, his Presence. This request sets in motion a second revelation to Moses of Yahweh's special nature. The first such request, made by Moses in his first meeting with Yahweh on Horeb/Sinai, prompted the revelation of the special name Yahweh, "the One Who Always Is," along with Yahweh's explanation of its meaning (3:13-14). This first request led to Yahweh's declaration "I AM, I REALLY AM," and the gift of the special name containing that confession.

The second request of Moses prompts Yahweh's own

description of *how* he *is*, a description that begins where the first response to Moses left off, with the special name, Yahweh. Thus at the beginning of the sequence of story in Exodus Yahweh declares to Moses, "I AM, and my name saying that is: Yahweh." And here at the conclusion to the sequence of story, Yahweh declares to Moses, "Yahweh! Yahweh! This is *how* I AM." These two special gifts of knowing are like brackets of revelation enclosing their own exposition, for nearly every line of the narrative between them illustrates them.

Yahweh is tenderly protective of Moses, arranging for him to ascend the mountain for the special revelation he is to receive, guiding him to a place of special shelter, and instructing him to prepare replacement tablets for the Ten Words, in anticipation of the renewal of Israel's shattered covenant relationship. Then, when Yahweh's instructions have been followed, and Moses is safely in the "fissure of the rocky cliff," Yahweh descends onto the mountain "in the cloud," passes in front of Moses, and calls out:

"Yahweh! Yahweh!
—a God compassionate and favorably disposed;
—reluctant to grow angry,
   and full of unchanging love and reliableness;
—keeping unchanging love for the thousands;
—taking away guilt and transgression and sin;
—certainly not neglecting just punishment,
   holding responsible for the guilt of the fathers
   both sons and grandsons,
   to the third and fourth generations." (34:6–7)

Moses' immediate response to this profound self-description by Yahweh was to bow low to the ground, prostrating himself in worship. No other response would seem appropriate. Simply reading this magnificent recital should be enough to prompt in any believer a similar response, since it is the one place in the entire Bible where God is represented describing himself in detail.

There is little reason to doubt that this description represents an ancient confession of belief about Yahweh. It is directly reflected in eight Old Testament passages (Num 14:18; Neh 9:17; Pss 86:15; 103:8; 145:8; Joel 2:13; Jon 4:2; Nah 1:3) and alluded to in other places in the Old Testament. Its summary listing, and the manner in which pieces and even phrases of it appear elsewhere in the Old Testament suggest that this description grew to its present form across many years, and was subject to alteration and expansion to fit varying circumstances. Its content here supports such a view, for the description handily summarizes the sequence of story in the book of Exodus.

Yahweh has been compassionate toward Israel in Egyptian bondage, and favorably disposed toward them, has rescued them and brought them to himself. Despite all their complaining, at the sea and in the wilderness and even at Horeb/ Sinai, he has been slow to anger and consistent in his unchanging love toward them. Now, despite the negation, from their side, of the covenant relationship, he has (by agreeing to continue along with them) taken away their guilt, their transgression, and their sin. Even so, for their own sake, he has taken seriously their disobedience of their own free promise, and is holding them responsible for it. They remain, though forgiven and disciplined, Yahweh's own possession, *his* people, despite their stubbornness, just as Moses asks (34:9).

Thus is it both possible and necessary for the broken covenant to be remade. This renewal Yahweh proceeds to initiate, not by a review of each of the Ten Words but by emphasizing the commandments (and specific applications of them) that have been violated in the making and the worshiping of the golden calf. Yahweh announces, "Look: I am making a covenant" (34:10). And the emphasis of this covenant is precisely the point at which Israel compromised the first covenant, absolute and undiluted loyalty to Yahweh, and to Yahweh alone.

For this reason, the very first direct command of this covenant-renewal sequence is a command to Israel to avoid compromising entanglements with the peoples who will be their neighbors in the land of promise (34:12-13). Following this command is a sequence of requirement (see pp. 93-95) that begins with the first two of the Ten Words, the two violated first of all in the making and the worship of the golden calf. The sequence moves on then to a summary series of seven requirements, directly linked to the kinds of compromise that would lead unavoidably to the violation of these first two of the Ten Commandments (34:18-26).

The covenant-renewal sequence ends with a command to Moses to write down these words (designed to prevent another golden-calf-type lapse) and with a note that Yahweh[24] wrote down on the stone tablets, once more, the Ten Words. No account is given of any ceremony of renewal parallel to the one described in Exod 24, but we may well assume that one took place, laying particular stress on total loyalty and commitment to Yahweh, whose "very name" is "Jealous," and whose jealousy is justified, because it is jealousy only of those who have made promises to him.

Such a report of a ceremony of covenant renewal would have made an appropriate ending to the sequence of story in the book of Exodus. The fact that no such ending is provided, we must remember, is primarily because the sequence of this story does not end with the end of Exodus, or of Leviticus, or even of Numbers.

The story of Israel's response to the revelation of God's Presence concludes with a kind of supplementary postscript reestablishing the authority of Moses as Yahweh's spokesman after the debacle of the golden calf. We are told that Moses, descending from Horeb/Sinai after his long period in Yahweh's Presence, had a shining face. So obvious was this condition that Aaron and the Israelites were frightened by him. When Moses called out to them, and then spoke to Israel's leaders without harmful results, Israel too approached him. Out of regard for the people's feelings, Moses began wearing a veil in their presence except when he was reporting to them some word from Yahweh. On those occasions, out of respect for Yahweh's Word and symbolizing the divine authority of the words he spoke, Moses left off the veil. The donning of the veil thus signified the difference between Moses' own words and those he reported from Yahweh.

Whereas Moses' first descent from Horeb/Sinai with the stone tablets containing Yahweh's Ten Words met with rejection and chaotic orgy, this second descent, with the new tablets, met with acceptance and an awed respect. Israel's response to Yahweh's Presence became once more both worshipful and obedient. For a while. Each one of us, in a quite personal way, knows both how long and, sometimes, at least, why.

God settles down in Israel's midst

There is one brief note more in the sequence of story in the book of Exodus. It comes following the final sequence of memory, which describes the implementation of Yahweh's instructions for the media of Israel's worship in his Presence. When Moses and those assisting him complete all the work of building the Tabernacle, its Court, its furnishings, and the priestly vestments and equipment, Yahweh's Presence fills the Tabernacle. This brief ending paragraph to the sequence of story in the book of Exodus is exultant, almost hymnic in nature. We are very nearly given the impression that Yahweh, eager to take up his residence among this people for whom and from whom he has suffered so much, comes rapidly but majestically into the place symbolizing his Presence, as soon as it is ready. And there in their midst, Yahweh guides his people Israel, in their travels and in their living.

3

THE SEQUENCE OF REQUIREMENT

As I have noted, at the end of chapter 1 and at the beginning of chapter 2, the sequence of story in Exodus has been pulled apart at appropriate points for the insertion of what I call sequences of *requirement* and sequences of *memory*. This rearrangement of what came to be the canonical form of our book of Exodus took place, in all probability, across a lengthy period of time and in successive layers related to the evolving need of the community of belief. It was done so brilliantly that the book of Exodus that has come down to us presents us with a quite remarkable unity. So remarkable is this unity, indeed, that we are tempted to think of Exodus, when we first begin to read it, as an uninterrupted continuum. We can almost understand the tradition that ascribed this text, along with the other four books of the Pentateuch, to Moses.

Upon a closer reading, however, the seams of the book of Exodus become more and more obvious to us. Different literary styles, distinctive sets of special terms, unique emphases, contrasting sets of particular concerns, repeated and conflicting versions of the same events, and the presence side by side of sections of narratives, sections of ceremony, sections of religious requirement, sections of social regulation, and sections of liturgical arrangement and symbol—all give us an increasing sense of the patchwork quilt appearance of Exodus.

At the same time, however, upon a sensitive reading of *all* of Exodus, or even large sections of it, we cannot escape an impression of wholeness, a certain sense of oneness, the unity that strikes us on a first reading. This unity is of course a unity of theme. Everywhere Exodus is a report and exposition of the theological theme, Yahweh's Presence among his people, among those who believe, at least some of the time, both that he *is* and is *here,* and who struggle, therefore, to live in accord with such a reality.

In the *Exodus* volume of the Word Biblical Commentary, I have attempted to examine Exodus in some detail in its component parts. In that same volume, however, I have also tried to present a translation and a commentary treatment that would present the thematic consistency of Exodus, and would make plain our need to think as carefully of the oneness of the book of Exodus that we have as we do of the variety of separate narratives, and legal and liturgical collections, that may have preceded it.

My concern in this compact survey is to emphasize this oneness of theme by presenting in sequence the three major types of material that are woven together in Exodus, each in its own separate sequence. This admittedly artificial apportionment of the text has three advantages:

- It enables us to perceive the full weight of each of the three components, apart from the interweaving of the other two.
- It enables us to see how consistently the one motivating theme of Presence governs each component, no

matter how different its separate styles and approaches.

- It gives us a clearer perception of the unity the canonical Exodus presents to us by showing how its separate parts work.

The sequence of story in the book of Exodus presents us with a narrative account of the revelation, the proving, the demonstration, and the presentation of Yahweh's Presence and a narrative account of Israel's response to that sequence of Advent. The sequence of story is thus above all a record of events. As event inevitably prompts reaction, so the event of Yahweh's coming and his subsequent invitation of Israel into covenant prompts reaction. That reaction is given guidance by a sequence of requirement, setting forth an application of the principles of living in the Presence of Yahweh. By "requirement" I mean to suggest all that is generally referred to by such terms as "law" (in both general and particular statement) and "commandment" (in both simple and expanded form). "Requirement" here is a general term, inclusive of the principles of life in covenant with Yahweh and the applications of those principles.

The events recorded in the sequence of story in the book of Exodus occur, of course, as all events do, only once in time. If the requirement that an event stimulates is to be kept by those who come after, the event must somehow be kept alive, a matter of the present rather than of the past. That, of course, is where the third component, the sequence of memory, comes into play. In no book of the Old Testament are these two additional sequences, crucially supplemental to the sequence of story, presented so effectively as they are in the book of Exodus.

There are three sequences of requirement in Exodus, and one brief section in the sequence of story describing how these requirements were applied. Each of the requirements listed is a specific response to the need of Israel to live and work differently because of the reality of Yahweh's Presence. Their declaration, no less than the declaration of the story of Exodus, is that God *is*, and *is here*.

How the requirements are applied to life

In the present arrangement of Exodus, a brief description of how Yahweh's principles for living in covenant with him are to be applied is given in the sequence of story when Israel first arrives at Sinai, even before Yahweh's self-revelation and giving of those principles. That description is included as a part of the narrative of the rendezvous of Moses and Israel with Jethro and Moses' family. The story has been discussed above, as a narrative of guidance. Of concern here is the description of how Moses is to apply Yahweh's principles for life in his Presence, a description given *before* the principles themselves are given, probably because of a need to present the Jethro traditions all in one place.

As we have seen already, Jethro, who has been mentor and man-in-charge to Moses, Aaron, and Joshua, critiques Moses' procedure in applying Yahweh's "requirements and instructions" to Israel's everyday problems. Upon his advice, Moses divides the problems being brought to him into two categories. He delegates authority for dealing with repetitive situations to a series of carefully selected "men of ability, who have reverence for God, men of firmness who hate a dishonest profit" (18:21). This division of the problems falls into "complex" problems and "routine" problems. The complex, which involve a new application of the "requirements and instructions" of Yahweh to a situation without precedent, Moses must deal with himself because the application may involve the consultation of Yahweh. The routine, for which such consultation is either unnecessary or has previously been made, can be handled by the "able men." Thus does Moses reduce both his own workload and the waiting period for those who wish to consult him. The resultant pattern of application is as follows:

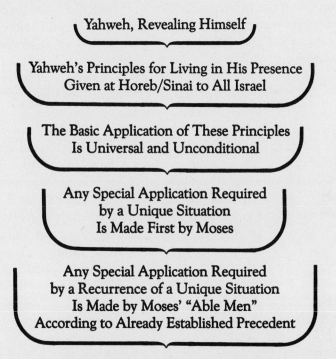

Yahweh, Revealing Himself

Yahweh's Principles for Living in His Presence
Given at Horeb/Sinai to All Israel

The Basic Application of These Principles
Is Universal and Unconditional

Any Special Application Required
by a Unique Situation
Is Made First by Moses

Any Special Application Required
by a Recurrence of a Unique Situation
Is Made by Moses' "Able Men"
According to Already Established Precedent

Israel, Yahweh's Covenant People

The movement of application is from the source of guidance, Yahweh, to those in need of guidance, Israel. The movement of guidance is from universal principles to the particular situation posed by a specific set of circumstances. The authority for guidance is ultimately Yahweh, but established solutions of guidance may be repeated continually if the conditions calling for guidance are the same. The entire process is operative because of, and under the inspiration of, Yahweh's Presence. Indeed, apart from that Presence the principles would be unnecessary, with neither source nor purpose. What we have here—set into the sequence of story describing the revelation, the proving, the demonstration, and the presentation of that Presence—is yet another attestation of the reality of that Presence. In all likelihood, it is an ancient tradition of the beginning of Israel's legal system.

Yahweh's principles for covenant life with his Presence

The Ten Commandments, in what I have described above (see pp. 58–63) as their compact original form[1] (the Ten Words mentioned in Exodus 34:28 and Deuteronomy 4:13 and 10:4) are a part of the sequence of story in Exodus. They are presented as a crucial part of the revelation of Yahweh's Presence at Horeb/Sinai. They are the words of Yahweh himself, heard not just by Moses, but by Israel along with Moses, when the people were assembled after careful preparation at the foot of the mountain. Any attempt to remove the commandments from the sequence of story or to relocate them is thus both misguided and misleading.

The commandments as they are presented to us in Exodus 20, however, are also a sequence of requirement *within* the sequence of story. They function as an integral part of the story of Horeb/Sinai, but they constitute, as well, the foundation for all of Yahweh's "requirements and instructions," his fundamental principles for life in covenant relationship with his Presence.

As they stand in the received text of Exodus, six out of ten of these basic principles have an expanded form, and the additions to them make quite clear that they were received and applied as fundamental requirements. These Ten Commandments are the principles for living in covenant that are given specific application in the largest sequence of requirement in the book of Exodus, "The Book of the Covenant" of 20:22–23:33.

The basic implication of these ten principles for living in covenant with Yahweh's Presence has been set forth already, as a part of the survey of the sequence of story. That basic implication has, however, been supplemented in the commandments that have been expanded, and this supplementation is strictly a part of the sequence of requirement and does not belong to the sequence of story.

Most extensively supplemented are the four commandments having to do with the primary aspect of Israel's existence, the relationship with Yahweh. It is understandable that these commandments were the ones most difficult to obey. They are still, because they require that God be given first place in our lives, absolutely and without reservation, and that everything connected with him in any way be taken seriously.[2]

Only God is to be god to those who enter into covenant with him (20:3). God must be taken on *his* terms alone; he will not present himself to us on our terms. We are not to impose on him a form, a concept, a behavior, or even a theology inconsistent with who and what and how he is. He is jealous, justifiably so, of those who have made promises to him. He takes us seriously and expects us to take him seriously (20:4–6). His name, the symbol of his Presence among us, must be treated with consonant respect; failure to do so is the equivalent of a failure of belief and will inevitably provoke punishment (20:7). The day of his rest, the sabbath, is to be a day set apart for holiness, for the recreation that joyful worship is. No labor is to be undertaken on that day, either directly or through some substitutionary person or animal. God rests on the seventh day and expects those in covenant with him to do so as well (20:8–11).

The six commandments guiding Israel's relationship with other members of the covenant community and with the human family beyond that community are not so fully expanded. This is in part, no doubt, because they were—with the exception of the fifth commandment and the tenth commandment—somewhat easier to obey. Despite their human direction, however, these commandments too are requirements of Yahweh, and keeping them honors him. The requirement of respect for one's parents, a requirement addressed primarily to adults (for whom parental care as well as child care is a basic responsibility), was apparently so poorly kept that it alone among the commandments came to have a reward tacked onto it. This supplement has a double edge: a long life for honoring one's parents, a short life for dishonoring them (20:12). Rebellion against one's parents could be a capital offense by Old Testament law (21:15, 17; Lev 20:9; Deut 21:18-21; 27:16).

The sixth, seventh, eighth and ninth commandments received no expansion. The tenth commandment, somewhat easier to abuse, received a supplement somewhat akin to that added to the fourth commandment, closing loopholes for abuse. In a way, indeed, the tenth commandment serves as a summary requirement, descriptive as much of an attitude as of a deed. Taken as such, it forms a kind of matching bracket to the first commandment: The first principle of life in covenant requires an uncompromising loyalty to Yahweh; this one requires an attitude of heart and mind that would close off much of the possibility of violating the other principles of life in covenant.

These ten basic principles of living in relationship with Yahweh's Presence thus set forth his fundamental expectations of his people, and so constitute, both logically and actually, the first sequence of requirement in the book of Exodus. The question of how these principles were to be applied to the circumstances and problems of everyday living is taken up by the second, and necessarily most complex, of the sequences of requirement.

The application of Yahweh's principles

The longest of the three sequences of requirement in Exodus has been inserted into the sequence of story immediately after the account of Yahweh's presentation of his Presence upon Horeb/Sinai and of his giving directly to Israel his ten principles for living in covenant with him. This location is entirely appropriate, since this collection of "guiding decisions" and "guiding principles" is a summary of concrete application of the principles stated by the Ten Words, made to meet the needs arising from the problems of everyday living.

These specific applications were arrived at and put into practice along the lines described in the narrative of Jethro's advice in Exodus 18:13-27. They are perhaps the clearest example in the Old Testament of the transition from the basic requirements of Yahweh's covenant law to the more specialized application of those requirements made necessary by the occurrence of particular situations of need.

Like such other collections of Old Testament legal material as the "Holiness Code" of Leviticus 17-26 or the wide-ranging laws of Deuteronomy 12-26, this "Book of the Covenant," so named from the reference of Exodus 24:7,[3] is a diverse collection. It reflects a wide range of contexts and probably the passage of a long period of time. It is made up of laws applying the principles of the Ten Words, and other principles derivative from them, to particular life situations. It also has laws setting forth entirely new principles connected with the Ten Words in only the most general ways. The first type, the case laws which we may call "guiding decisions," make up most of the first half of the collection, roughly 21:1-22:17.

The second type, the universally applicable laws we may call "guiding principles," make up most of the second half, roughly 22:18-23:19. The entire collection is not given unity by any commonality of literary form or subject matter, however, but by its presentation as guidance originating in Yahweh and by its single purpose, the shaping of Israel's life in covenant with Yahweh's Presence.

A pointed indication of this unity of origin and purpose is given in the beginning of this lengthy sequence of requirement, with its clear reference to Yahweh's presentation of his Presence on Horeb/Sinai and its specification of the divine authority for the entire collection:

> So Yahweh said to Moses, "Here is what you are to say to the sons of Israel: 'You yourselves have seen that from the heavens I have spoken with you.'" (20:22)

A further indication of this same unity is made by the beginning (20:23) and the ending (23:32–33) of the entire collection, each of which is, in content and application, a summary of the first two principles set forth in the "Ten Words."

I have set forth in my commentary (WBC 3) a detailed analysis and explanation of the Book of the Covenant.[4] My purpose here is to deal with the "guiding decisions" and "guiding principles" as reflections of the Presence and Response-to-the-Presence themes that govern the sequence of requirement in the book of Exodus, just as they govern also the sequence of story and the sequence of memory. That many of these laws are an application to specific situations in Israel's life is obvious. Some commentators, indeed, have worked out lists of equivalents.[5]

Too rigid a connection of the Ten Words to this diverse collection is a mistake, however. The primary bond between the two lies in the guidance they offer Israel for living in response to Yahweh's Presence among them. Whether a given "guiding decision" or a given "guiding principle" can be linked to a given commandment is, in the final analysis, quite irrelevant. Every part of the sequence of requirement is from the same source and to the same end.

Thus the instructions about the building and the use of altars (20:24–26) are intended to guard against the diluting influence of syncretism. The collection of "guiding decisions" related to the treatment of slaves and the establishment of their rights (21:2–11) is a reflection of Yahweh's concern for every human being. The collection dealing with harm done to others, whether it is brought about deliberately or through negligence, and whether it results in death or injury (21:12–36), is an indication of Yahweh's desire for concord and harmony among those in covenant with him. The collection concerned with property—whether livestock, crops, money or other possessions, including virgin daughters (22:1–17)—is connected with Yahweh's demand for honesty in all relationships among his people (cf. 20:17).

The three offenses for which the death penalty is specified (22:18–20) each represent an attack upon Yahweh himself, the first by an attempt to escape or alter his will, the second as a sexual deviation reflecting syncretism, the third as a violation of the first of the Ten Words.

The collection of "guiding principles" sympathetic to the cause of the defenseless "newcomer," the widow, the orphan, or the poor is a reminder that Yahweh, in Israel's midst, will hear the distressed cries of such persons and "will be furious" (22:21–27). This theme is sounded repeatedly by the great prophets of the eighth and seventh centuries. Of course, Israel is not to "make light" of God by ignoring his "guiding principles," by showing disrespect for a leader in the covenant community, by holding back from Yahweh's use that to which he is entitled, or by eating food improperly gained. Since Yahweh among them is holy, so also must they be holy (22:28–31).

The collection of "guiding principles" and "guiding decisions" that begin the final chapter of this lengthiest of the sequences of requirement is also concerned with ethical and humane behavior. Like 22:21-27, it addresses honest testimony in legal matters, humaneness toward animals, even those belonging to an enemy, and fair treatment of "newcomers" (23:1-9). Yahweh present among Israel demands of them truth, honesty, and kindness. The requirement of seventh-year rest for the land, and seventh-day rest for Israel, their slaves, their "newcomers," and their animals is of course an expansion of the principle of the fourth commandment. It is a recognition of Yahweh at hand and pausing that they might pause (23:10-12).

Exodus 23:13 is a kind of summary requirement, a restatement in a way of the first commandment. It functions therefore as a conclusion to the "guiding decisions" and the "guiding principles." The requirements that follow it amount to a supplementary addendum dealing with the calendar of the sacred festivals (23:14-17) and with miscellaneous instructions related to sacrifices and offerings (23:18-19).

The three sacred festivals are linked to the three climactic ingatherings of the agricultural year: the first grain harvest (of the winter barley), the early crop harvest (of wheat and spelt) seven weeks later, and the final autumnal harvest (of all the crops). On each of these occasions, every Israelite male was "to appear in the Presence of the Lord, Yahweh" (23:17), in testimony of his Presence among them in the giving of the bounty of the crops. The miscellany dealing with sacrifices and offerings is an even more specific application of the first of the Ten Words than 23:13, which introduces this addendum.

The final section (23:20-33) of this longest of the three sequences of requirement functions as a kind of epilogue to the entire Book of the Covenant. It is much broader than the conclusion it is sometimes made out to be, for its orientation is toward Yahweh, and undiluted loyalty to Yahweh, rather than toward the preceding collection of requirements.

Its emphasis is upon serving and worshiping Yahweh alone (23:20-24). It looks forward to the fulfillment of the second part of Yahweh's covenant-promise in the settlement of the land promised to the Fathers, a land to be vacated by Israel's competitors gradually (23:27-30), a land the borders of which are the expanded borders of Davidic-Solomonic glory (23:31). Thus the theme of this ending of the Book of the Covenant is, like that of its beginning in 20:22-23, the application of the guiding principles laid down in these first two of the Ten Words. And the warning accompanying this explanation is that any openness, in any manner, to the other gods available to Israel for worship, will lead to entrapment, disobedience, and failure (23:24, 32).

Yahweh's restatement of his principles

This sequence of requirement is largely repetitive, in that most of the principles listed in it or inferred by it have been given already in either the Ten Words or in the Book of the Covenant. Its difference from what we are given elsewhere lies largely in its focus. That focus is one of context: This sequence has been woven into the narrative of Israel's first disobedience of the covenantal commitment as an account of the renewal of the shattered covenant relationship. Its orientation, therefore, is dictated by the circumstances of disobedience which first led to the violation of Israel's covenantal commitment. Thus this sequence emphasizes total loyalty to Yahweh (as opposed to the disloyalty of making and worshiping the golden calf). It deliberately pulls together the principles from the Ten Words and the application of them in the Book of the Covenant that would prevent the kind of disloyalty Israel had just shown.

The first, the second (34:14-17), and the third (34:21) of the commandments are stressed, and the keeping of the calendar of the harvest festivals (34:18, 22-24, 26a) which involve an acknowledgement of Yahweh as provider, in Yahweh's Presence. The temptation to give credit to the agricultural deities of Israel's neighbors is thus ruled out, as is the temptation to honor their fertility deities: The firstborn of flock, of herd, and of each family in Israel belongs only to Yahweh present among them (34:19-20). They are to keep leaven from the sacrifices and respect the special sanctity of Passover (34:25), and they are not to boil a kid in its mother's milk (34:26b), both requirements protective against syncretistic influence.

Some of the requirements listed here replicate in verbatim (or near-verbatim) form requirements listed in 23:12-19. And the emphasis here, as there, is upon a complete, uncompromising loyalty to Yahweh. Thus when Yahweh says, at the beginning of this sequence, "Look: I am making a covenant" (34:10), and at the end of it, to Moses, "you yourself write these words, for on the basis of these words I have made a covenant with you and with Israel" (34:27), we are being given a directed renewal, a renewal shaped by the disobedience that has disrupted the covenant relationship and made its renewal a necessity. This emphasis is further underscored by the recurrence (see 20:5) of the motif of Yahweh's justified jealousy:

"Indeed you are not to bow down in worship to another god, because Yahweh's very name is 'Jealous': he is a jealous God." (34:14)

Once more in relation to Yahweh's covenant requirements, the fulfillment of the promise of land is anticipated, and with a double implication. The promise will be fulfilled to those in an obedient covenant relationship with Yahweh's Presence—but they are to guard themselves carefully against any alliance with the people already living in that land which might prompt them once again to a shattering of their covenantal promises to Yahweh (34:14-16).

"These words" which Moses is to write down as a basis for making yet again a covenant, by Yahweh and for Israel (34:27), are specifically the focused words of renewal, directed to the point of the disruption: Israel's divided, compromised loyalty. More broadly, of course, all the words, of both principle and application, of law and covenantal living by it, are summed up in that phrase.

And this third and last of the sequences of requirement in the book of Exodus ends as the very first of them began, with a reference to the ten principles of Yahweh for life in covenant with his Presence:

He wrote upon the tablets
    the words of the covenant,
the Ten Words. (34:28c)

4

THE SEQUENCE OF MEMORY

Exodus, like the rest of the Bible of which it is a part, may be said to have begun in an event, an event that led in turn to a sequence of events. The report of that event and the other events it prompted became the sequence of story that forms the framework of Exodus. The event of Exodus, of course, is the coming of the Presence of Yahweh, the "One Who Always Is."

That event, and its report, in turn, gave rise also to a sequence of requirement, a series of expectations guiding the response of Israel to the revelation that *the God who is, is here*. These expectations, set forth as both common obligations and also as obligations unique to special situations, amount to a validation of the report of event. They do so because the keeping of requirement is the surest evidence that the report of the event has been believed, and that the event has thus been taken seriously.

The revelation of Yahweh's Presence to Moses on Horeb/ Sinai led to a proving of the reality and power of that Presence to Israel and to the Egyptians. That proof was supported by a demonstration of Yahweh's Presence to

Israel in the wilderness, and it was brought to a dramatic and powerful climax by the theophany to all Israel at Horeb/ Sinai. An integral part of that theophany to Israel was the revelation of the ten principles of living in response to Yahweh's Presence here among us; and that revelation became the basis of an array of guidance in applying the ten principles to problems of daily life. Revelation stimulated response, and response needed requirement to guide it. The "law of Moses," in both its general and its specific statement, is the summary of that requirement, the road map for journey in covenant with Yahweh.

Event thus led to report, and report became the basis of expectation. Those who reported the event, to begin with, were those who had experienced it. And they were the ones for whom a response, of some kind, was inevitable. Even the negative response of the golden calf was yet a response.

But what of those of generations still to come—those for whom the bad times in Egypt, the Exodus from oppression, the deliverance at the sea, the provision in the wilderness, and even the theophany and the awesome speaking at Sinai would be someone else's story? Why should they respond, to a covenant they had not made? How could they see a deliverance they had not shared as *their* deliverance, and how could the Presence so real to those who had gone before them be real also to them? It is, in a way, the pressing question of every faith in any time, the necessary and constant preoccupation of every leader of worship, whether pastor, priest, or parent.

The answer to these questions lies in what Martin Noth has called "actualization" or "re-presentation."[1] Re-presentation is remembrance and renewal through confession of faith, through the retelling of the story of the events of faith, through the ceremonies and the symbols of worship. As Noth has put it, "'Re-presentation' is based then on this: that God and his activity always *are*, here and now, though human beings, in their unavoidable temporalness, cannot comprehend this here and nowness except by re-presenting the activity of God again and again in their worship."[2] As Deuteronomy 5:2–3 puts it,

"Yahweh our God contracted with us a covenant at Horeb.
Not merely with our fathers did Yahweh contract this covenant—
rather with us, we ourselves, those right here, all of us living right now!"

This same insistence is present in the revelation to Moses of the name Yahweh, the name that above all symbolizes God's Being and Presence, the name about which Yahweh says "This is my name from now on, and this is to bring me to mind generation after generation" (Exod 3:15d). "Yahweh" is to be God's *zeker*, the "remembrance" that will make his Presence real to the generations of Israel yet to come. Such is the point also of Psalm 111:4, which declares: "Remembrance [*zeker*] creates his extraordinary deeds."

There are seven sequences of memory in the book of Exodus, each in its own separate way presenting an array of reminders, all of them supplemental to the sequences of story and requirement. These sequences of memory are intended as catalysts of re-presentation, designed to actualize as here and now the past events that provoke present faith. The memories they call up, and sometimes even create, have the effect of making events in time timeless. These memories— names heavy with history, rituals summarizing crucial times and events, hymns reviewing the past and leaning into the future, visible symbols of Yahweh's constant nearness—are each and all a means of making event real and so of making requirement not only justified but also a happy privilege. They function in ways similar to the favorite texts and hymns of our worship. Or, at a much higher and more solemn level, they function as does the reflection of Holy Week, or the Communion of the Lord's Supper, or the joy of the worship of Advent and Christmas Eve.

The single continuous and persistent reminder of the book of Exodus, and indeed of the entire Old Testament, is of course the tetragram itself, the name Yahweh, the "One Who Always Is," occurring some 6,823 or more[3] times throughout the Old Testament. Every time this name was seen, every time it was pronounced,[4] it was a confessional re-presentation of the God *who is* and *is here*.[5] Indeed the sequence of the story of Yahweh's deeds and the sequence of the statement of Yahweh's requirements, often repeated, became both an illustration of the meaning of the name *Yahweh* and a means of re-presentation. The poetic summary of covenant theology now located in Exodus 19:4-6, and no doubt employed as a set piece for ceremonies of covenant renewal, serves as an example:

"You yourselves have seen what I did to the Egyptians,
and that I then lifted you upon wings of eagles
and brought you to myself.
So now, if you will pay very careful attention to my
voice,
and keep my covenant,
then you will be my own special treasure
from among all peoples
—for to me belongs the whole earth—
and you yourselves will be my own kingdom of priests
and holy people."

Two lists of special names

The first two of the seven sequences of memory in the book of Exodus are lists of names, lists that on a first reading may seem to have only a remote connection with the sequence of story or the sequence of requirement in Exodus. The first of them gives to Exodus its Hebrew title, $w^e elleh$ $sh^e mot$, "and these are the names." The second of them is an obvious attempt to legitimize Aaron, by tracing in detail his lineage from Levi. Both lists may well strike the reader of the English text as largely unpronounceable and eminently skippable.

These lists, however, deserve a closer look. The names they record frequently have a theologically confessional significance all their own. The lists themselves are a reflection of the intense interest of ancient Israel's theological historians and worship leaders in having the right people in the right place at the right time, and in charge of things. But most of all, these lists present us with two interlinked sequences of memory, a theological-historical means of re-presenting, as here and now, Israel's significant religious past.

A partial listing of the names that clearly have a theological meaning will establish the first point:

Reuben	"Behold, a son!" (connoting a special blessing in the Old Testament),[6] 1:2
Simeon	"He Surely Heard!"
Levi	"Joined"
Joseph	"Increasing One," 1:5
Yachin	"He Makes Firm," 6:15[7]
Shaul	"Asked For"
Amram	"Exalted People," 6:18
Yitshar	"First Oil"
Chebron	"Uniter"
Uzziel	"My Might Is El"
Yochebed	"Yahweh's Honor," 6:20
Zikri	"My Remembrance," 6:21
Mishael	"Who Is That Is God?," 6:22
Eltsaphan	"God Has Treasured"

Sitri	"My Hiding Place"
Elisheva	"My God Is Seven," 6:23
Abihu	"My Father Is He"
Eleazar	"God Has Aided"
Elqanah	"God Has Created," 6:24

As for the second point, the list in Exodus 1:1-5 includes the names also listed in the summaries of Genesis 35:22-26, 46:8-27, 49:3-27, and Deuteronomy 27:12-13 (compare also Deuteronomy 33:2-29, which is missing the name of Simeon). This list emphasizes the direct descent from the patriarchal Fathers themselves to the generation sojourning in Egypt, the proof of Yahweh's Presence there, and the Exodus through the wilderness to Horeb/Sinai—the mountain of his nearness, his guidance, and his covenant with Israel.

These twelve tribal fathers are each the great-grandsons of the Father in faith himself, Abraham, the grandsons of Isaac, and the sons of Jacob/Israel. A more legitimate line of predecessors could hardly be imagined, for these sons are the beginning of the fulfillment of the promise of a vast progeny, and they are themselves the fathers of the generation who are to see the beginning of the fulfillment of the promise of land. These twelve sons are the bridge from the Fathers to the future. By the time they die, that future, promised over and over to Abraham, has already become the present: Israel's progeny has become "a teeming swarm."

Indeed, they became so many they were a strength to be reckoned with by their numbers alone. The land was simply filled with them. (Exod 1:7)

And, as Galatians 3:29 makes plain, these fathers in faith are, through faith, our fathers too.

The list in Exodus 6:14-27 confirms this legitimacy still further. It traces the genealogy of the first two sons of

Jacob/Israel through their first generation, and the genealogy of the third son, Levi, through his first three generations (to Aaron and Moses), and the genealogy of Aaron through his second generation, to Pinchas.

This concentration on Aaron, himself presented as in "the seventh generation from Abraham" (counting Abraham as the first generation of Yahweh's call), is of course an attempt to lend authority to the house of Aaron, as the preeminent priestly family. But the much larger purpose of this list here is to embrace both Aaron and Moses as appropriate descendants of the covenant-promise to Abraham, Isaac, and Jacob, Moses and Aaron being absolutely the right people in the right place at the right time, taking the charge given them by Yahweh himself.

More important still is the presentation of these two lists as interlinked sequences of memory. Each of them brings the past into the present and impels the present toward the future. They do so not only by the listing of the names of those who have come before the Exodus, those who have in Yahweh's multiplying Presence become a vital part of making the Exodus a necessity. They also do so by listing the names of those who would lead that Exodus, and be present at, and a vital part of, the birth of Yahweh's special possession, his priestly and holy people. These leaders bring that people into the future Yahweh is opening, a future Abraham had been told would hold a blessing for "every family of the earth" (Gen 12:3), a company that includes us.

For Israel, every one of the names had its own special importance, calling the past into the present by the memory of faces and of faith, of adventures, of deeds, of sacrifices, of miracles. The fact that the names that are known to us— Abraham, Isaac, Jacob/Israel, Reuben, Levi, Judah, Joseph, Benjamin, Aaron, Moses—are fewer in number by no means alters these lists as a stimulus to keeping the story and honoring the requirements of faith. They are like the names of those members of our own families who have made us what we are. The simple calling out of such names, even in the silent hearing of our hearts, is enough to make the past present, and the future a greater privilege and greater responsibility.

Family names, given names, nicknames, names of intimate familiarity—they are the most effective sequence of memory of all, for they call to our present not merely event but personhood, not just example but heritage, not only remembrance of persons past but necessity in the present moment.

And these are the names . . . (1:1)

Thus did the boy grow. His mother . . . called his name "Moses." (2:10)

Then Moses said, "Show me, please, your glory."
Yahweh replied, "I will call out the name Yahweh
in your presence." (33:18–19)

He took his place beside him there, and he called
out the name, Yahweh. (34:5)

And the angel said to her, ". . . you are to call his
name Jesus." (Luke 1:30–31)

Therefore God . . . gave him the name above every
name, that at the name of Jesus every knee
should bow, in heaven, on earth and in the deep,
and every tongue confess, "Jesus Christ is
Lord, to the glory of God the Father."
(Phil 2:9–11)

Two rituals of remembrance

The related requirements of the ritual of Passover and Unleavened Bread and the dedication to Yahweh of every firstborn life in Israel function in Exodus as requirements of recollection. They have been inserted into the sequence of story as sequences of memory (as have the lists of names of 1:1-5 and 6:14-27) at those points in the story that provide their justification. Their purpose, then, is to call from the past to the present that story, to make the fathers' Exodus experience the Exodus experience also of the sons and the sons' sons, down all the generations. Their parallels, in our own remembrance in and for worship, are the service of communion and the service of the dedication (or christening or baptism) of newborn children.

This note of recollection is sounded within the two sequences themselves. Of Passover/Unleavened Bread, the text says, "This day is to be for you a day of remembering. You are to observe it, a day sacred to Yahweh, generation after generation: you shall observe it as a requirement forever" (12:14). Of the dedication to Yahweh of every first-born life, the text says,

> "Keep in mind this day in which you went out from Egypt, from the non-status of slaves, because by strength of power Yahweh brought you out thence. . . . You shall explain to your son on that day as follows: 'This is because of what Yahweh did for me in my coming out of Egypt.' And it is to be for you a sign upon your hand and a reminder between your eyes, in order that the instruction of Yahweh may be in your speech, because with a strong power Yahweh has brought you forth from Egypt. So you are to keep this requirement at its scheduled time year after year." (13:3, 8-10)

The origin of the Passover meal of a flock animal in a nomadic spring festival and the origin of the eating of unleavened bread cakes in a spring harvest festival have been frequently pointed out.[8] It is not the origin of the observance of

Passover/Unleavened Bread that is of first importance here, however. While such a tradition was certainly an asset to the keeping of these requirements, the purpose for keeping them, firmly fixed in the re-presentation of the Exodus experience, was that the successive generations of Israel might remember, and so bring that experience from the past into the present. The Passover, to be celebrated in "the first of the year's months," was a memory of the meal carefully, but hastily, prepared and eaten with unleavened bread cakes and bitter herbs. The main course of this meal was a yearling male of the flock, either a lamb or a goat, from which also some blood was used to mark "the two doorposts and the lintel they support" of the houses where Israel dwelled.

The unleavened bread cakes were a symbol of the haste necessary in the preparation of this meal—note the sequence of story at Exodus 12:34:

> So the people took up their dough before it could rise; their breadboards were wrapped up in their coats and carried upon their backs.

With this reference it is instructive to compare the report, at Exodus 12:39, of what happened at the first stop in the journey of the Exodus:

> At the first stop, they baked the dough which they had brought from Egypt into round, flat, unleavened bread-cakes—it had not risen, because they were pushed out of Egypt and had no chance to linger, indeed they had packed no food for themselves.

The bitter herbs were in memory of the bitter experience of the oppressive bondage in Egypt.

The consecration in Israel of every first-born life, of the human family or of the herd or the flock, is a second ritual of remembrance connected with the Exodus experience. Like Passover/Unleavened Bread, this ritual too appears to have had an ancient, pre-Exodus origin, perhaps even in connection with human sacrifice. In the sequence of memory in the book of Exodus, however, it has been linked to Israel's obligation to make a grateful response to Yahweh's protection of Israel's firstborn during the devastation of Egypt's firstborn. In Exodus 13:3–10 the instructions given in 12:14–20 are substantially repeated, as a part of the specifications connected with the sacrifice or the substitutionary replacement of the firstborn. This expensive requirement, too, was a means of bringing the Exodus experience from the past into the present, as a timeless act of the perpetually present Yahweh:

> "It is necessary, when your son asks you, in due course, 'What is this?' that you say to him, 'With a strong power, Yahweh brought us out of Egypt, from the non-status of slaves. For when Pharaoh was stubborn-minded about sending us forth, then Yahweh killed all the firstborn of the land of Egypt, from human firstborn to the firstborn of domesticated animals. For that reason, I am sacrificing to Yahweh all the males that open the womb, except all my firstborn sons, whom I am replacing.'" (13:14–15)

The detailed specification regarding these rituals of remembrance, and their establishment as requirements of Yahweh forever, make plain that they were seriously regarded. It is hardly fortuitous that each of the two major elements of the Passover meal had a prehistory separate from the other. Their combination, in this one festival, linked the separate festive occasions of two distinct occupations, that of the nomadic flock keepers and that of the settled land cultivators. But their function in combination was to stimulate the memory of faith, in the time of the year that has always spoken of new life and new beginnings. The flock animal thoroughly roasted and consumed by a household (12:3-4), the taste of unleavened bread cakes and bitter herbs, the accompanying recitation of the story of the tenth mighty act and the Exodus it provoked, after so much disappointment—this ritual of remembrance was so that a new generation might taste and smell and feel the anxiety and euphoria of the fathers' deliverance as *their* deliverance.

The costly requirement of every firstborn life, likewise, was so that the successive generations of Israel might realize with gratitude the seriousness of their obligation to Yahweh. This second ritual gave Israel a taste of the Exodus experience in a different dimension of life. First, a hasty meal, with bread made quickly, and with a taste of bitter along with a taste of sweet; second, a perpetual requirement of ransom from oppression. In such a manner, Yahweh's past Presence will always continue as Yahweh's Presence now. We should not be surprised that Jesus made these rituals of remembrance the basis of our own Christian re-presentation of his Passion on our behalf, or that the church has made so much of "the Lamb of God, who takes away the sin of the world," or that we should confess a grateful belief in the vicarious suffering of "the first-born of all creation." In this way we know Easter to be reality here and now and for us, an event that happens as fact in our lives on the first day of every week.

Three hymns of remembrance

No sequence of memory in worship is likely to lack a poetic and musical dimension. The singing of God's praise is certainly a vital part of the worship of ancient Israel, as the book of Psalms alone is sufficient to show. It is, therefore, no surprise that Yahweh's powerful Presence in the constitutive event of Israel's faith would be celebrated in a hymn of eclectic form which was expanded across the years to celebrate additional events regarded as testimony to his Presence.

The point of origin for this hymn is undoubtedly Yahweh's deliverance of Israel at the sea:

> "I will sing to Yahweh,
>   for he has risen proudly:
> horse and chariot alike
>   he has cast into the sea!"
>   (Exod 15:1, 21)

At least this stanza, and perhaps also some part of the first of the three hymns woven here into one can be taken as contemporary in origin with the deliverance being celebrated.

This point of departure, however, is simply a beginning medium for the message of Exodus, that the incomparable Yahweh is dramatically and effectively present among his people. In a way, this hymn in three parts is a summary of the foundational theological premise of all of Exodus and, therefore, of the Old Testament as well: Yahweh's sovereign Presence rescues, protects, and establishes those who, by faith, would be his own people.

The bulk of the hymn (15:1b–12), as we would expect, given its setting, is concerned with Yahweh's delivering Presence at the sea. Its two supplementary divisions deal respectively with the guidance of Israel, by Yahweh's Presence, through the wilderness (vv 13a, 14–16) and with the leading of Israel to the place where his Presence dwells in holiness (vv 13b, 17–18).

Each one of the three hymns presents Yahweh as entirely incomparable:

First hymn: "Who is like you among the gods,
                            Yahweh?

Who is like you,
   magnificent in holiness,
   awesome in praiseworthy deeds,
   doing the extraordinary?" (v 11)

Second hymn: "The peoples have heard—
   they are worried. . . .
Terror and dread have fallen over
   them—
against the greatness of your arm,
they are struck dumb as stone."
   (vv 14a, 16)

Third hymn: "Yahweh reigns forever
   without interruption." (v 18)

In close connection with this emphasis, a recurrent one in the Old Testament, the special name of Presence, Yahweh, the "One Who Always Is," is sounded as a dominant chord. In the first line of the first hymn (15:1) and in the last line of the third hymn (v 18), this confessional name is set; and counting these two occurrences and the shorter form Yah in verse 2, the name is sounded ten times in the eighteen verses of the three hymns.

In addition, it is the antecedent of no fewer than thirty-six pronouns in the same eighteen verses. Altogether, that is forty-six references to Yahweh in eighteen verses—small wonder that verse 3b declares, "Yahweh is his name!"

Yahweh is the name of his incomparability: The fact that he *is*, and *is here*, and always *is*, and always *is doing things for his people*—these attributes make Yahweh unlike any of the gods worshiped by Israel's neighbors, and in their times of incomprehensible lapse, by Israel's people themselves.

Thus does the first hymn (15:1b–12), the foundation for this composite celebration of the powerful Presence of Yahweh in Israel, sing the song of Yahweh's great victory over

Pharaoh's formidable force at the sea. Pharaoh is represented as confident of his victory over Israel (v 9), but he is swept aside by Yahweh, who manipulates not only the waters and currents of the sea, but even the "ancient deeps" that he brought under control in the creation of the world (vv 5, 8).[9]

The second hymn (15:13a, 14–16), in logical sequence, commemorates the guidance of Israel through the wilderness and through an array of competing peoples, all of whom, despite their undoubted military prowess, are described as being overcome by weak-kneed anguish when they hear of the mighty arm of the incomparable and unconquerable Yahweh. The third hymn (15:13b, 17–18) concludes the confessional recital by celebrating the arrival of Israel at Zion, the new Sinai, the place of Yahweh's dwelling among his people in the great Temple built by Solomon in David's city, Jerusalem.

A series of additional motifs interlace this composite poem, each of them attesting Yahweh's incomparable Presence among his people. His control of the primordial deep, his defeat of the Pharaoh (who is sometimes connected with the chaotic deep), and his stunning impression of the peoples who might oppose Israel are supplemented by other references. These recall his action toward Israel as a redeeming kinsman (see also Exodus 6:5–8) and his creation of Israel as his own people, his "firstborn son" (4:22), "established" by him in the promised land to which he has brought them (15:17). And finally, this entire tapestry of themes is capped by a reference to the continuing and uninterrupted kingship of Yahweh, his permanent rule (15:18).

So three hymnic memories, each of a different and successive mighty accomplishment of Yahweh's Presence, have been woven together in rhythmic re-presentation of the Exodus experience. As we have seen, that experience was made necessary by the fulfillment of the first part of Yahweh's covenant-promise to the Fathers. Then in turn, the Exodus made necessary the movement into the promised land and into the new Sinai, Mount Zion in Jerusalem, in fulfillment of the second part of that covenant-promise. How many times over this poem was recited, and sung in worship, we cannot calculate. Each of those times, however, Yahweh ("the One Who Always Is Here") was remembered. He still is. We remember Yahweh and the revelation of his Presence in the sequence of story in the book of Exodus, when we sing "Rock of Ages, Cleft for Me"—just as we bring to mind Christ and his Passion when we sing "O Sacred Head, Now Wounded." Our singing, no less than Israel's, is a re-presenting sequence of memory.

The places, the objects, the persons, the acts of remembrance

The concluding sequence of memory in the book of Exodus is a sequence of thirteen chapters. It is inserted into the sequence of story as a series of Yahweh's instructions for the media of Israel's worship in his Presence (25:1–31:18) and as a report of Israel's obedience to those instructions (35:1–40:33). These two parts of this sequence of memory are logically placed into the sequence of story. The instructions immediately follow the account of Israel's entry into covenant with Yahweh, and the obedience of those instructions follows the account of the renewal of that covenant after the disobedience with the golden calf. While the two sections deal necessarily with many of the same concerns, and are therefore inevitably repetitive, they are not the mirror-image parallels they are sometimes made out to be. Their repetitions have a didactic purpose, their sequencing is logically different, and their emphases reflect separate approaches to a single theme.

Indeed, a more appropriate conclusion to the book of

Exodus than the one provided by this lengthy sequence of memory can hardly be imagined, because it presents in so single-minded a manner *the* fundamental theme of Exodus, the Presence of Yahweh. For this reason, despite the length of the sequence and the often painstaking detail of the instructions given in its thirteen chapters, it can be given thematic summary in fairly brief compass.

The two parts of the sequence are an extended preparation for the worship of Yahweh by the people who have covenanted with him and with each other to live in his Presence. Their premise is worship as confession. They begin with a call for an offering of special materials for the manufacture of the symbols, the spaces, and the equipment of that worship (25:1-9; cf. 35:4-9). They end with an announcement of the satisfactory completion of all the work instructed by Yahweh (40:1-33).

The two parts of the sequence and also the book of Exodus itself are then brought to conclusion by a solemn report of the one moment toward which the combined sequences of story, requirement, and memory have all been moving: the settlement in Israel's camp of the glorious Presence of Yahweh (40:34-40). It is an entirely apt conclusion that is at the same time a beginning, for the final phrase of Exodus is a reference to Yahweh's Presence now with Israel "throughout all their journeyings."

The first section of this sequence of memory moves forward from the assumption that, following the acceptance of the conditions of the covenant with Yahweh, Israel must make preparation for his residence among them. "They are to make me a holy place," says Yahweh, "and I will dwell in their midst" (25:8).

This theme is the recurrent, almost obsessive, motif of the entire section, which moves in a logical progression from the instructions for the making of the Ark to the instructions for the implements kept near the Ark, to the plan for the sanctuary and most holy shelter of the Presence (the Tabernacle). Next the section moves to the Altar of Burnt Offerings outside the Tabernacle, and the Tabernacle Forecourt in which it is placed, to the special vestments of the priests and the directions for their authority-giving preparation, to a miscellany dealing with special accessories of worship, with the artisans who are to make them all, and with the special worship occasions of atonement and sabbath.

The second section begins where the first one left off, with the sabbath, and the artisans who are to perform the labor of manufacture. It then moves to the narrative of construction (which mentions first the Tabernacle, and then the Ark and the implements of the Presence kept near it), then to the equipment of the Tabernacle Court and the Court itself. Finally (following a summary of the metals used in the Tabernacle and its Courtyard), the section moves to an account of the making of the sacral vestments, to a summary of the fulfillment of Yahweh's instructions and an account of the setting up and the consecration of the Tabernacle and the cleansing of the priests in preparation for worship.

The constant theme throughout the thirteen chapters of the two sections, the motif symbolized and depicted and celebrated in every conceivable way, is that Yahweh, who *is*, *is here*. No space, no object, no material, no person, and no movement is mentioned anywhere in these chapters that is not a reminder of Yahweh's Presence. We are presented here with architecture as worship and with movement as liturgy, with objects and motion as remembrance and re-presentation. It is a lesson we have largely lost, and one we need urgently to relearn. Our church buildings are too devoid of remembrance and too preoccupied with practicality, and the sacerdotal presence in our services of worship is altogether too person- and personality-oriented.

Each structure, each space, each object, each person, each act in this sequence of memory serves as a reminder of the basic point of the sequence of story in the book of Exodus and as justification of each expectation in the sequence of requirement. The materials to be used in making the media of worship were to be only the best available, were to be given freely (25:1-9, paralleled by 35:4-9), and *were* given, so joyously and so abundantly that a halt had to be called when the amount of gifts became so excessive that they created an obstruction (35:1-36:7). And at the very end of this extensive accumulation of remembrance, Yahweh comes, settling upon the array of reminders, imbuing them with his glory.

The Ark and the Ark-Cover (25:10-22, paralleled by 37:1-9) represented the place of supreme focus for Israel's attention to the Presence of Yahweh: Where the Ark was, Yahweh promised to meet Moses "by appointment," and said, "I will speak with you, from above the Ark-Cover, from between the two cherubs upon the Ark of the Testimony" (25:22). "The Table of the Presence" (Num 4:7) was an object near the Ark on which were to be placed containers for bread, incense (Lev 24:7), and wine (25:23-30), suggesting Yahweh's Presence in the gift of sustenance. The Lampstand (25:31-40), with its bud-and-bloom symbolism and its seven burning lamps, was a reminder of Yahweh's Presence everwakeful and life-giving (compare Jeremiah 1:11-12 and Psalm 121:4 and probably also Numbers 17:1-11). Each of these objects most intimately associated with Yahweh's Presence was either overlaid with pure gold or made entirely of it.

The Tabernacle, the shelter for these opulent reminders of the Presence, was similarly made of the best available materials, but was to be arranged in two sections of nearness (26:1-37). Its Holiest Space, the place where the Ark and the Ark-Cover were positioned, was to be set apart by an elaborately embroidered curtain. Within and near this Holy of Holies only the most precious and rare materials were used;

farther from it, in the Holy Space of the remainder of the Tabernacle, special (but less precious and rare) materials were used. Even the movement into the holiness of the Tabernacle was in this way surrounded by a heightened and increasing awareness of Yahweh's Presence. The Tabernacle was to stand in the center of Israel's camp, and within that Holy Space was a Holiest Space, made unmistakable by the rising value of the materials leading to it and into it.

The construction of this Tabernacle, however, gave yet another important reminder: It was entirely portable, and could be conveniently relocated. Yahweh's Presence was not to be considered stationary. Israel was in covenant with a moving Presence. It is an emphasis of remembrance that we would do well to imitate, given our tendency to isolate God and matters religious from our daily living, and our relegation of them to the church buildings we visit only at carefully scheduled times.

The Altar (27:1–8) and the Tabernacle Court surrounding both it and the Tabernacle (vv 9–19) are of course similarly portable, and a further suggestion of the movement toward and away from the most intimate space of Yahweh's Presence. The metal accessories and overlay of this altar were to be made of copper, as were the pedestals supporting the shielding draperies of the Tabernacle Court. Anything (and of course anyone) coming close to Yahweh's Presence must always be good, better, best. This too is an emphasis of recollection we very much need.

The Holy Spaces and their furnishings having been described, the sequence of memory moves next to a description of the elaborate vestments and the ordination of the priests. By their ministry of worship they joined the three circles of nearness to Yahweh: the Tabernacle Court, the Holy Space, and the Holiest Space of the Tabernacle itself. The priests, referred to as Aaron and his sons, were yet another reminder of Yahweh's Presence. Their vestments

(28:1–43, paralleled by 39:1–31) were specifically symbolic of that Presence:

> The Ephod of gold, the material used most often for the objects closest to Yahweh's Presence, includes also the engraved onyx-stones through which Israel was to be brought to mind in Yahweh's Presence. The Breastpiece of Judgment, attached to the Ephod, was through its twelve engraved gemstones to keep Israel before Yahweh and to signify the glow of the Presence through Israel. The Urim and the Thummim placed inside this Breastpiece were to suggest Yahweh's judgment and specific direction of his people. The Robe of the Ephod was a reminder of Yahweh's plenty and nearness, and the engraved Flower on the Turban was a reminder that Israel and all that Israel undertook were set apart to Yahweh—made what they were by him and in need of becoming what they were called to be in his Presence. In sum, every article of the sacral vestments made the same point, each with its own specific accent: Yahweh Is here, we are his, and we must both know this and show this.[10]

These priestly vestments were designed specifically to call the worshipers' attention to the object of, and so the reasons for, worship. They disguised the worship leader's personality instead of calling attention to it. They were, rightly, a denial of the self-puffing tendency so obvious in so many places where the worship of God should be taking place.

The authority-granting ordination of "Aaron and his sons" (29:1–46, paralleled by Lev 8:1–33), likewise, was also an attestation of Yahweh's Presence, in his provision for Israel's sustenance, both physical and spiritual. Indeed, this section ends with a remarkable summary of the promise of Yahweh's Presence sounded in the first nineteen chapters of Exodus, turning the "proof of the Presence" narratives in the sequence of story into a "Presence-giving proof" confession in the ministry of worship in Yahweh's Presence:

"So I will dwell in the midst of the sons of Israel, and I will be their God, and they will know that I am Yahweh their God who brought them forth from the land of Egypt on account of my dwelling in their midst. I am Yahweh their God." (Exod 29:45-46)

Following the chapters of instruction for the building of the Ark and the Ark-Cover, the Table, the Lampstand, the Tabernacle, the Altar, the Tabernacle Court, for the making of the vestments of the priests, and for the ordination of the priests, there are three appendices, giving further instructions regarding the preparation of Israel for worship in Yahweh's Presence.

The first appendix deals with four accessories to that worship: (1) the Golden Altar of the Special Formula Incense (30:1-10, paralleled by 37:25-28), (2) the "most holy" incense to be used on it (30:34-38), (3) the Bronze Laver for Ceremonial Ablutions (30:17-21, paralleled by 38:8), and (4) the Special Formula Anointing Oil (30:22-33).

The golden incense altar and the special and expensive mixture burned upon it were further indications of the uniqueness of the Holiest Space of Yahweh's Presence, before which the altar was placed and the special incense was burned. The special and expensive oil for anointing the furnishings of worship and the priests was also a testimony of the difference made necessary by Yahweh's Presence, as was the Laver for Ceremonial Ablutions: The priests were to wash their feet before approaching the Tabernacle in which were the special symbols of focus of Yahweh's Presence, and they were to wash their hands before handling the implements of his Presence. The instructions for the payment of the atonement money (30:11-16) appear to have been located in the middle of this first appendix because of Israel's need to provide for the upkeep of the Tabernacle, its furnishings, and equipment.

The second appendix is a report of Yahweh's designation of the artisans who are to undertake the work specified by his instructions for the media of worship (31:1–11, paralleled by 35:10–19; 35:30–36:1). The artisan in charge is to be Bezalel, whose name means "In El's protecting shadow," and whose native ability Yahweh has augmented with additional wisdom, discernment, and skill. Bezalel is to have an assistant, Oholiab, who is similarly to have a divine enhancement for the complex work at hand, as also are all the workmen to be employed. As only the best materials are appropriate to the worship of Yahweh's Presence, so also only the most artistic minds and the most skilled hands are appropriate to undertake the molding of these materials.

The third and final appendix is a list of instructions for the keeping of the sabbath (31:12–18, paralleled by 35:1–3). This list, a considerable elaboration of the fourth commandment, is an appropriate conclusion to the first seven chapters of this longest sequence of memory, in its reminder of the requirement of a day regularly set apart for remembering Yahweh and what it means to be his people. The sabbath was to become "a sign" between Yahweh and Israel, "a perpetual covenant," "a sign in perpetuity" (31:13, 16–17). As Yahweh himself "rested and so caught his breath" on the seventh day (31:17), so Israel was to do, that they might remember and better know his Presence.

The second section of this longest of the sequences of memory reports, as we have seen, the fulfillment of Yahweh's instructions for the media of worship in his Presence. The materials called for were given by Israel in complicating abundance. Then the Tabernacle, with its furnishings and equipment, and the Tabernacle Court, and its equipment, were duly built.

The metals used in this work amounted to astonishing totals, a lavish testimony to the importance given to symbolizing the nearness of Yahweh's Presence: Approximately 2,210 pounds of gold, 7,601 pounds of silver, and 5,330 pounds of copper are reported (38:24-29).[11] The weaving, sewing, and decoration of the sacral vestments of the priest are described, with a sevenfold repetition (39:1, 5, 7, 21, 26-27, 31) of the statement that this work was done "exactly as Yahweh had commanded Moses," and a final summary of the fulfillment of all Yahweh's instructions is made, using much the same phrase (39:42-43).

Then, at last, the Tabernacle was set up and its furnishings arranged, and Aaron and his sons were anointed to their special work of worship. A stimulus had been provided for each of the five senses in the range of the acts of worship these priests were to carry out. No avenue of memory is neglected in the construction of the Tabernacle and its equipment, in the authorization and attire of the priesthood, and in the acts of worship they were to offer and to guide—acts described in minute detail in Leviticus. In every conceivable way, the Tabernacle, its Courtyard, their furnishings and equipment, and the vestments of the priest are a multi-media declaration of the fundamental theme of the book of Exodus,[12] the Presence here of the "One Who Always Is." So also should the places and the persons which stand at the center of our worship be a remembrance of the Presence, the mercy, and the saving activity of our God— the "One Who [still] Always Is."

There does not exist in the Bible a book more permeated with its purpose or more consistently and constantly an expression of its theme than the book of Exodus. The announcement that God *is, here*, is made, in one way or another, in its every paragraph, and very nearly in its every sentence. It is an announcement of wide-ranging implications, and yet it is a confession summed up in the single four-consonant name YHWH, Yahweh, the "One Who Always Is."

At the beginning of the book of Exodus, indeed in its very first verse, we are given the report of a journey of Jacob/Israel's twelve sons. They went down into Egypt, in a journey we can remember, from the sequence of story in Genesis, as one guided and accompanied by Yahweh. The heart of Exodus describes another journey, undertaken by a much-multiplied Israel—and also guided and accompanied by Yahweh—out of Egypt to Yahweh's special mountain, Horeb/Sinai. There, as never before, Israel learned what Yahweh's companionship meant. And so at the end of the book of Exodus, still further journeyings beckon—but they too will be undertaken with the guidance and in the company of Yahweh, the "One Who Always Is."

He is, still, this guiding and accompanying God, and *he is*, still, *here*. No one of us has to live beyond or without his Presence. That, at last, is the theme of the book of Exodus. Small wonder that Yahweh should keep calling out to us "The One Who Always Is! The One Who Always Is!" (Exod 34:6)—despite manifold evidences to the contrary, we still have difficulty believing him, just as Israel did so many proofs ago. Yet he *is*, still, and he is still *here*. Before life, within life, beyond life, he is still. And if the center of our worship were different, and our knowledge of the sequences of story and requirement and memory in the Bible were more complete, and if our behavior were more an acknowledgement of his will than of our wants, we would know that he is and that he is here.

Thus does God cry out to us still, "The One Who Always Is! The One Who Always Is!" And thus does he wait for our response, given honestly as well as earnestly, "He is, and he is risen! The Lord is risen indeed!"

The Sequence of Memory   121

NOTES

Chapter 1   The Theme of Exodus: God Is Here

1. Compare the suggestion of Michael Goldberg, *Jews and Christians Getting Our Stories Straight: The Exodus and the Passion-Resurrection* (Nashville: Abingdon Press, 1985), 26: "The story also tells us right from the start that it is more than just a story about Israel; as a *master story*, it is about all humankind."

2. See especially the summary statement, "The Book of Exodus as a Whole," xix–xxiv.

3. See the brief summaries in *Exodus*, WBC 3, pp. xxvi–xxxiv and the eighty-three pericopae bibliographies, *passim*.

Chapter 2   The Sequence of Story

1. Northrop Frye, *The Great Code: The Bible and Literature* (New York: Harcourt Brace Jovanovich, 1982), 171.

2. "On the same principle the resurrection of Christ, around which the New Testament revolves, must be, from the New Testament's point of view, the antitype of the Exodus." *Ibid.*, 171–72.

3. See for example Harald Sahlin's article, "The New Exodus of Salvation According to St. Paul" in *The Root of the Vine*, ed. Anton Fridrichsen (London: A. and C. Black, 1953), 81–95, and Bernhard W. Anderson's "Exodus Typology in Second Isaiah," in *Israel's Prophetic Heritage*, ed. B. W. Anderson and W. Harrelson (New York: Harper and Brothers, 1962), 177–95.

4. Note the fascinating theory of Michael Goldberg, who calls the Exodus narrative "the Jewish master story" that both informs and forms the lives of human beings in *Jews and Christians Getting Our Stories Straight: The Exodus and the Passion-Resurrection* (Nashville: Abingdon Press, 1985). And compare the approach of J. P. Fokkelman, who says the Exodus "provides a foundation for the whole Bible" in "Exodus" in *The Literary Guide to the Bible*, ed. Robert Alter and Frank Kermode (Cambridge: The Belknap Press of Harvard University Press, 1987), 56–65.

5. Michael Walzer, *Exodus and Revolution* (New York: Basic Books, 1985).

6. See "Exodus: From J to K, or the Uncanniness of the Yahwist," in *Congregation: Contemporary Writers Read the Jewish Bible*, ed. David Rosenberg (New York: Harcourt Brace Jovanovich, 1987), 9–26.

7. See *Exodus*, WBC 3 (Waco, Tex.: Word Books, 1987), 27–41.

8. See *The Art of Biblical Narrative* (New York: Basic Books, 1981), 131–54.

9. Frye, *op. cit.*, 161–62.

10. In *The Elusive Presence: Toward a New Biblical Theology* (New York: Harper and Row, 1978), 110–50.

11. Francis Brown, S. R. Driver, and Charles A. Briggs, eds., *A Hebrew and English Lexicon of the Old Testament* (Oxford: Clarendon Press, 1952), 1027–28.

12. "Exod 3:14: History, Philology and Theology." *Catholic Biblical Quarterly* 40 (1978): 311–22.

13. In "Exodus," *op. cit.*, 63.

14. Frye, 17.

15. In "The Revelation of the Divine Name YHWH" in *Proclamation and Presence*, eds. John I Durham and J. R. Porter. New corrected edition (Macon, Ga.: Mercer University Press, 1983), 70–71.

16. See the extensive summary review of Tryggve N. D. Mettinger, *In Search of God: The Meaning and Message of the Everlasting Names*, trans. by Frederick H. Cryer (Philadelphia: Fortress Press, 1988), 14–49.

17. See further WBC 3, pp. 45–46.

EXODUS

18. As for example in the patriarchal stories of Genesis 12, or the history of Israel in and beyond the Babylonian exile.

19. For a helpful survey of this important theme, see C. J. Labuschagne, *The Incomparability of Yahweh in the Old Testament* (Leiden: E. J. Brill, 1966).

20. See *Exodus*, WBC 3, pp. 238-53.

21. So reads the Septuagint; the Masoretic text has "God" (*'Elohim*).

22. For a detailed consideration of the "jigsaw-puzzle appearance" of Exodus 24, see *Exodus*, WBC 3, pp. 340-48.

23. See more fully on this point *Exodus*, WBC 3, pp. 416-19, 426-28, 435-36, 440-42, 445-46, 450-52, 458-60, 465-66.

24. The text says, "He wrote"—for a justification of my view that Yahweh, not Moses, is the antecedent of this pronoun, see *Exodus*, WBC 3, pp. 457, 462-63.

Chapter 3 The Sequence of Requirement

1. See more fully the summary review of Eduard Nielsen, *The Ten Commandments in New Perspective*, Studies in Biblical Theology 7, second series. Transl. D. J. Bourke (London: SCM Press, 1968), 78-93, and Walter Harrelson, *The Ten Commandments and Human Rights* (Philadelphia: Fortress Press, 1980), 33-42.

2. John I Durham, "Christians and the Ten Commandments," *Advanced Bible Study* (a publication of the Sunday School Board of the Southern Baptist Convention, Nashville, Tenn.), vol. 7, no. 4, (July-September 1977), 39-125.

3. See also the references in 2 Kings 23:2, 21; 2 Chronicles 34:30, which probably refer to some part, probably a large part, of the book of Deuteronomy.

4. See *Exodus*, WBC 3, pp. 305-37.

5. See, for example, Delbert R. Hillers, *Covenant: The History of a Biblical Idea* (Baltimore: Johns Hopkins Press, 1969), 89-97, and, more generally, Nahum M. Sarna, *Exploring Exodus: The Heritage of Biblical Israel* (New York: Schocken Books, 1986), 130-89.

Chapter 4 The Sequence of Memory

1. Noth's article, which appeared originally in *Evangelische Theologie* 12 (1952), 6-16, can be found in English as "The

'Representation' of the Old Testament in Proclamation" in *Interpretation* 15 (1961), 50–60 and in C. Westermann, ed., *Essays on Old Testament Hermeneutics* (Richmond, Va.: John Knox Press, 1963), 76–88.

2. *"Die Vergegenwärtigung des A.T. in der Verkündigung,"* *Evangelische Theologie* 12 (1952), 13.

3. See *Exodus*, WBC 3, pp. 287–88.

4. Note Exodus 3:15–16; 33:19; 34:6–8; Numbers 6:22–27; see *Exodus*, WBC 3, pp. 39–40, 452–54.

5. See pp. 20–28, and note the comment of Tryggve N. D. Mettinger, *In Search of God: The Meaning and Message of the Everlasting Names*, transl. F. H. Cryer (Philadelphia: Fortress Press, 1988), 40: "We could perhaps affirm that the biblical divine Name expresses *the conviction of God's active and helpful presence*, not as an expression about the past, but rather as a statement of confidence about the present and future: 'He Is [here and is now helping].'"

6. On the meaning of this name, and of the other eleven sons of Jacob/Israel, see *Exodus*, WBC 3, pp. 4–5.

7. For the meanings of all the names in the list of 6:14–25, see *Exodus*, WBC 3, pp. 80–83.

8. See the extensive survey of "The Primitive Passover" of J. B. Segal, *The Hebrew Passover, from Earliest Times to A.D. 70* (London: Oxford University Press, 1963), 155–88.

9. For a fuller treatment of this important point, see *Exodus*, WBC 3, pp. 199–207, and the bibliography cited there.

10. *Exodus*, WBC 3, p. 390.

11. On the calculation of these totals, see *Exodus*, WBC 3, pp. 490–91.

12. See, for a fascinating and detailed summary of this point, Menahem Haran, *Temples and Temple-Service in Ancient Israel* (Oxford: Clarendon Press, 1978), 149–259.

SELECTED BIBLIOGRAPHY

Buber, Martin. *Moses: The Revelation and the Covenant.* New York: Harper and Brothers, 1958.

Childs, Brevard S. *The Book of Exodus.* Old Testament Library. Philadelphia: Westminster Press, 1974.

Daube, David. *The Exodus Pattern in the Bible.* All Souls Studies, II. London: Faber and Faber, 1963.

Durham, John I. *Exodus.* Word Biblical Commentary, vol. 3. Waco, Tex.: Word Books 1987.

Goldberg, Michael. *Jews and Christians Getting Our Stories Straight: The Exodus and the Passion-Resurrection.* Nashville: Abingdon Press, 1985.

Haran, Menahem. *Temples and Temple-Service in Ancient Israel.* Winona Lake, In.: Eisenbrauns, 1985. Originally published by Oxford: Clarendon Press, 1978.

Harrelson, Walter. *The Ten Commandments and Human Rights.* Philadelphia: Fortress Press, 1980.

Herrmann, Siegfried. *Israel in Egypt.* Studies in Biblical Theology, second series, 27. Translated by Margaret Kohl. London: SCM Press, 1973.

Hillers, Delbert R. *Covenant: The History of a Biblical Idea.* Baltimore: Johns Hopkins Press, 1969.

Hyatt, J. Philip. *Exodus.* New Century Bible. London: Oliphants, Marshall, Morgan and Scott, 1971.

Knight, George A. F. *Theology as Narration.* Edinburgh: Handsel Press, 1976.

McCarthy, D. J. *Old Testament Covenant: A Survey of Current Opinions.* Richmond, Va.: John Knox Press, 1972.

Mettinger, Tryggve N. D. *In Search of God: The Meaning and Message of the Everlasting Names.* Translated by Frederick H. Cryer. Philadelphia: Fortress Press, 1988.

Nicholson, E. W. *Exodus and Sinai in History and Tradition.* Richmond, Va.: John Knox Press, 1973.

Sarna, Nahum M. *Exploring Exodus: The Heritage of Biblical Israel.* New York: Schocken Books, 1986.

Segal, J. B. *The Hebrew Passover, from Earliest Times to A.D. 70.* London Oriental Series, 12. London: Oxford University Press, 1963.

Terrien, Samuel. *The Elusive Presence: Toward a New Biblical Theology.* Religious Perspectives, 26. San Francisco: Harper and Row 1978.

deVaux, Roland. *Ancient Israel. Vol. 2: Religious Institutions.* Translated by John McHugh. New York: McGraw-Hill, 1965.

Walzer, Michael. *Exodus and Revolution.* New York: Basic Books 1985.

Zimmerli, Walther. *I Am Yahweh.* Translated by Douglas W. Stott. Atlanta: John Knox Press, 1982.

INDEX OF SCRIPTURES